ABSTRACTS

OF THE

EARLY DEEDS

OF

CLEVELAND COUNTY, OKLAHOMA

Book 1
June 1889 – July 1893

Ann Jacobs

and

Lisa Sheppard

HERITAGE BOOKS
2021

HERITAGE BOOKS

AN IMPRINT OF HERITAGE BOOKS, INC.

Books, CDs, and more—Worldwide

For our listing of thousands of titles see our website
at
www.HeritageBooks.com

Published 2021 by
HERITAGE BOOKS, INC.
Publishing Division
5810 Ruatan Street
Berwyn Heights, Md. 20740

International Standard Book Number
Paperbound: 978-1-58549-810-9

These abstracts represent the information contained in the first book of deeds for transfers between individuals of property in Cleveland County, Oklahoma. The time span is roughly from June 1889 to July 1893. The information as listed in this volume represents the book and page number of the deed, the name(s) of the grantor/seller, grantee/buyer, date of the contract, date of filing if noted, property description, type of instrument, pertinent commentary contained in the deed, and any witnesses listed on the original deed. Many deeds had only one date, which is presumed to be the date of the contract. Many deeds had no witnesses other than the local recording clerk or notary public, whom we did not list. We have been very literal in transcribing the names of all parties exactly as shown in the original instruments. As the book includes the handwritten records of numerous individual clerks, these vary a great deal. Following the abstracts is an index of every person listed in the deed abstracts, and an index of places referred to.

1:8   Pulman, R.A. to Rose, Robert Jun;
       24,1890; Sep 18, 1890; Lots 8 &
       9 Blk 88 of Norman, OT; Quit
       Claim Deed;   Grigsby, J.D.

1:9   Joyce, Robert & Leavy, Samuel T. &
       Hay, Daniel;   Certificate #510
       Oct 1, 1890; Oct 14, 1890; SE4& W2
       of SW4 of Sec 29 & Sec 30 T9N
       R2W   Town Plat of Norman, OT.

1:11   Jones, George F. & Minnie M.(wife)
       to Allen, Mary E.; Nov 8, 1890; Nov
       8, 1890; Lot 9 Blk 13 of Norman,
       OT.

1:12   McKinnis, Jackson P. & Mrs. Lena
       E. (wife) to Bender, Peter A.;Nov
       24, 1890; Nov 25, 1890; SE4 Sec 28
       T11N R2W; Mortgage; Warranty
       Deed.

1:14   Chilson, W.D. & V.B. (his wife) to
       Eslick, John; Dec 3, 1890; Dec 3,
       1890; Lots 17, 18, 19, 20, Block 16
       of Norman, OT; Warranty Deed;
       Rood, C.L. & Hennessy, E.E.

1:16   Gordon, Samuel W. & Addie to
       Synnot, Ellen & Aniol, Robert;
       Dec 2, 1890; Dec 5, 1890; 2/3
       interest in SE4 Sec 29 T9N R2W
       containing 39.65 acres; Warranty
       Deed; Cook, T.R.

1:18   Branhan, John, Estate of, W.H.
       Seawell admin. to Hardwick, William
       Dec 8, 1890; Dec 8, 1890; Lot 25,
       Block 13 in Norman, OT; Warranty
       Deed; Chilson, W.D.

1:20   Leeper, W.P. & M.W. (wife) to
       Brittain, M.L.; Nov 29, 1890; Dec
       11, 1890; Lots 18 & 19, Block 5 in
       Norman, OT; All parties are
       residents of Tery, Cleveland County,
       OT; Warranty Deed; Robert, M.W.
       & McCollum,W.

1:22   Berry, Addie & Berry, Andrew A.
       (wife & husband) to Fisher, A.W.
       Dec 15, 1890; Dec 16, 1890; Lot 24,
       25, 26, 27 & 28, Block 3, "village of
       Norman, OT"; Warranty Deed;
       Rood, C.S. & Cease, Frank P.

3

1:24 Dunham, Frank (single man) to
Zysett, John; Dec 12, 1890; Dec 18,
1890; SE4 Sec 32 T11N R3W;
Zyett from Richardson Co.,
Nebraska; Warranty Deed; Hull,
D.H. & MacMartin, D.F.

1:25 Ragon, R.B. to Ragon, E.B.
Blachard (his wife); Nov 21, 1890;
Dec 22, 1890; Lots 29, 30, 31 & 32,
Block 20, City of Norman, OT;
Warranty Deed; Adamson, W.B.

1:26 Ragon, R.B. & E.B. Blachard (his
wife) to Eslich, John I.; Dec 12,
1890; Dec 12, 1890; Lots 29-32,
Block 20, city of Norman, OT;
Warranty Deed; Stanley, J.S. notary.

1:28 Waggoner, Nettie (wife of T.R.
Waggoner) to Waggoner, T.R.;
Jan 7, 1891; Jan 7, 1891; W2 NE4
(part of Waggoner Addition), City
of Norman, OT; Sec 31 T9N R2W;
Warranty Deed; Rood, Mrs. C.L. &
Galbraith, C.

4

1:29   Blake, Tyler to Blake, Mary E.;
        Nov 11, 1890; Jan 8, 1891; Lots 5 &
        6, Blk 16 & Lots 19 & 20, Blk 12,
        Lot 32, Blk 13, Lot 15, Blk 5, Lots 3
        & 4, Blk 23, Norman, OT; Warranty
        Deed; Reed, Fred.

1:30   Wood, John B. widower to Duck,
        John; Jan 6, 1891; Jan 16, 1891;
        Lots 1 & 2 and S2 NE4 Sec 1 T10N
        R4W; Warranty Deed; Flick, D.W.
        & Flick, Taylor.

1:31   McPhee, William J. & Alice Maude
        (his wife) to McGinley, John &
        Frank J.; Jan 10, 1891; Jan 23,
        1891; Lot 12, Block 14, city of
        Norman, OT; McPhees residents of
        Dickinson Co., Kansas; Quit claim
        Deed; McMillan, George A.

1:32   Steen, John & F.C. (husband & wife)
        to Frick, James; Jan 24, 1891; Jan 26,
        1891; E2 NE4 Sec 26 T11N R4W;
        Warranty Deed; Wedder, Perry &
        Newton, C.M.

1:34   Pressgrove, Wenfield S. & N.J. (his

5

wife) to Labegger, Mary Almeda;
Jan 21, 1891; Jan 26, 1891; NW4
Sec 33 T11N R2W; N.J.
Pressgrove cannot write; Warranty
Deed; Elgin, Charles H. &
MacMartin, D.F.

1:36   Howard, George H. (a single man) to
        Cox, James D.; Jan 26, 1891; Jan 27,
        1891; SE4 Sec 17 T10N R4W;
        Warranty Deed; Jennings, R.H.&
        Reed, Fred H.

1:37   Jones, Dora & Ed H. (husband &
        wife) to Fisher, W.B.; Dec 15, 1890;
        Feb 2, 1891; Lots 8, 9, & 10, Block
        2, Norman, OT; Warranty Deed;
        Rood, C.S. & Cease, Frank R.

1:38   Trustees Methodist Episcopal
        Church: J.E. Turner, W.S. Choate,
        J.P. Jackson, W.T. Wallace to Innis,
        Robert E.; Jan 29, 1891; Feb 6,
        1891; Lots 15 & 16, Block 15, town
        of Norman, OT; Warranty Deed;
        V.A. Wood, B.B. Blakeney, T.J.J
        Wiggins, F.J. Orrick, T.R. Cook,
        Richard Hill, J.S. Briscoe.

1:40   Mitchell, John (a single man) to
        Schmick, E.O.; Feb 7, 1891; Feb 7,
        1891; NE4 Sec 18 T9N R2W; John
        Mitchell cannot write; Warranty
        Deed; Cook, Thomas R.

1:41   Walcher, Benjamin I. to Jones,
        James A.; Feb 19, 1891; Feb 19,
        1891; Lot 9, Block 14, town of
        Norman, OT; Warranty Deed;
        Estill, Tuen & Hennessy, E.E.

1:42   Hales, George H. & Mary F. (his
        wife) to Massey, James W.; Feb 12,
        1891; Mar 2, 1891; SW4 Sec 31
        T11N R3W; George H. Hales
        cannot write; Warranty Deed; Reed,
        Fred H. & Carson, J.M.

1:43   Waggoner, T.R. & Nannie (his wife)
        to Wallace, W.T.; Feb 17, 1891;
        Feb 27, 1891; S2 W2 NE4 Sec 31
        T9N R2W, Also includes numerous
        town lots in the Waggoner Addition,
        Norman, OT; Warranty Deed.

1:45   Easton, Henry C. to Easton, Ellen G.;
        Mar 7, 1891; Mar 19, 1891; SE4 Sec
        33 T 7N R1W; Warranty Deed;
        Cossey, A.J. & Goodin, J.W. &
        Countiss, A.P.

1:47   Steen, John & F.C. (husband & wife)
        to Blackburn, W.C.; Mar 4, 1891;
        Mar 7, 1891; W2 NE4 Sec 26 T11N
        R4W; Blackburn from Oklahoma
        County, OT; Warranty Deed;
        Ransom, Charles W.

1:48   Wallace, W.T. & M.E. (his wife) to
        Beldeu, Julia; Feb 27, 1891; Mar 11,
        1891; Lots 31 & 32, Block 86,
        Waggoner Addition of Norman, OT;
        Warranty Deed; A.T. Ross, notary.

1:49   Bowling, C.G. & Alice (his wife)
        to Owens, S.B.; Mar 14, 1891; Mar
        16, 1891; NE4 Sec 29 T9N R2W;
        Fox affidavit affecting this note; see
        Book 15, misc. page 146; Warranty
        Deed.

1:51   Trustees of city of Noble; Leavy,
        Samuel T; Joyce, Robert; Hay,

8

Daniel;Certificate #83, US; Feb 25,
1891; Mar 13, 1891; SE4 & NE4
Sec 27 T8N R2W, 320 acres,
township of Noble, OT.

1:53   Wallace, Wiley T. & Mary E. (his
       wife) to Poole, W.B.; Mar 16, 1891;
       Mar 20, 1891; Lot 4, Block 72,
       village of Norman; Warranty Deed;
       A.T. Ross, notary.

1:54   Owens, S.B. & Etta (wife) to
       Marquart, D.W. & M.E. & G.E.;
       Mar 16, 1891; Mar 20, 1891; Lot
       13, Block 14, & Lot 6, Block 22,
       Norman, OT;   Mortgage.

1:56   Wallace, W.T. & M.E. (wife) to
       Richardson, T.M.; Mar 17, 1791;
       Mar 17, 1891; Lots 29, 30, 31, & 32,
       Block 15, Waggoner Addition to
       Norman, OT; Warranty Deed.

1:57   Wallace, W.T. & M.E. (wife) to
       Richardson, W.C.W.; Mar 17, 1891;
       Mar 21, 1891; Lots 22-32, Block 17,
       Waggoner Addition to Norman, OT;
       Warranty Deed; A.T. Ross, notary.

9

1:58   Rose, Robert & Jane (wife) to
        Meacham, Charles W.; Mar 19,
        1891; Apr 6, 1891; Lot 8 & 9, Blk
        88, Norman. OT; Warranty Deed;
        MacMartin, D.F.

1:60   Peck, W.H. & Francis J. (his wife) to
        Anderson, W.A;. Mar 31, 1891;
        Apr 13, 1891; Lots 16, Block 6,
        Norman, OT; Warranty Deed;
        T.J. Rollins, M.L. Johnson.

1:61   Bowling, C.G. & Alice (his wife) to
        Forbes, C.G.; Apr 4, 1891; Apr 13,
        1891; NE4 Sec 29 T9N R2W, 42
        acres; Warranty Deed.

1:62   Bowling, C.G. & Alice (his wife) to
        Trustees of Methodist Church South:
        Averyt, A.N.; Chastain, J.M.;
        Jackson, J.P.; Turner, J.E.; Seawell,
        W.H;. Apr 4, 1891; Apr 4, 1891;
        NE4 Sec 29 T8N R2W;10 acres for
        the Oklahoma High School of the
        Methodist Church South; Warranty
        Deed; A.W. Fisher, notary.

1:64   Andrew, Cassues W. (unmarried) to

Cartwright, Mary J.; Apr 7, 1891;
Apr 15, 1891; NE4 Lots 7 & 8, S2
NE4 Sec 3 T7N R2W; Warranty
Deed; Cartwright, L.J. &
Waggoner, T.

1:65   Arnold, Wootson & Mary H. to
       Hudson, L.P.; Apr 8, 1891; Apr 16,
       1891; Lots 3, 4 & 5 & SE4 NW4
       Sec 6 T 10N R2W; Hudson resident
       of Oklahoma County, OT; Warranty
       Deed.

1:67   Hudson, Louis P. & Sarah J.
       (husband & wife) to Curtice, J.M;
       Apr 8,1891; Apr 16, 1891; Lots 3, 4,
       & 5 & SE4 NW4 Sec 6 T10N
       R2W; Hudsons & Curtice residents
       of Oklahoma Co., OT; Warranty
       Deed.

1:69   Grove, Michael B. to Andrew,
       Casseus W.; Feb 28, 1891; Apr 16,
       1891; Lots 1-16, Block 7, & Lots 1-
       16, Block 8, Lots 1-16 Block 21 all
       plat of Noble, OT; Warranty Deed;
       Rennie, Albert & Hutchin, A.

11

1:71   Newland, John to Wallace, W.T.;
        Feb 21, 1891; Apr 20, 1891; Lots 8-
        10, Block 67 in Norman, OT; note
        additional affidavits; Record Book 2
        page 339; Warranty Deed.

1:72   Wallace, W.T. & M.E. (husband &
        wife) to Burroge, J.C.; Apr 20,
        1891; Apr 21, 1891; Lots 8-10, Blk
        67, in Norman, OT; Warranty Deed.

1:73   Griffin, Thomas & Exa (husband &
        wife) to Burroge, J.C.; Apr 21,
        1891; Apr 22, 1891; Lots 24, 25 &
        26 Blk 32 in Norman, OT; Warranty
        Deed.

1:74   Keller, E.J. (single man) to
        Bondurant, J.D.; Mar 30, 1891;
        Apr 27, 1891; Lots 8 & 9, Block 57,
        Lot 20-32 Block 81, City of
        Lexington, OT; Keller of Oklahoma
        County, OT; Bondurant of Jefferson
        County, Kentucky; Warranty Deed;
        Belcher, W.H & Davis, Robert A.

1:75   McKinley, D.T. to McKinley,
        Dorothy (his wife); Jan 20, 1891;

Apr 27, 1891; Lots 23, Blk 22, town of Norman, OT; McKinleys residents of Lucas Co., Iowa; Warranty Deed.

1:76 Easton, Henry C. & Ellen G. (husband & wife) to Shannon, Martha T.; Apr 6, 1891; Apr 29, 1891; Lots 25, Blk 43, town of Lexington with 16'X16' house; Shannon resident of Hamilton County, Kansas; Warranty Deed; Haws, F.W.

1:77 Belcher, Mack (widower) to Adams, M.L.; Apr 7, 1891; Apr 30, 1891; Lots 1 & 2, & S2 NE4 Sec 2 T10N R2W; Warranty Deed; Vance, J.M., notary.

1:78 Hardrick, William (unmarried man) to Andrew, Casseus W.; Apr 7, 1891; Apr 30, 1891; NE4 Lots 7 & 8, S2 NE4 Sec 3 T7N R2W; Warranty Deed; Cartwright, L.J. & Waggoner, T.

1:79 Stewart, James & Harriet E. (husband & wife) to Jennings,

Amanda J.; Apr 7, 1891; Apr 30,
1891; NW4 Sec 20 T10N R4W;
Warranty Deed; Fisher, K.S. &
Elgin, Charles H

1:80   Isbell, John to Thiel, Peter J.; Apr 4,
1891; May 1, 1891; Lots 1-16, Block
63 town of Noble, OT; Warranty
Deed; Huron, E.E. & Elkins, J.A.

1:82   Rixse, Ed C. to Smith, George;
Apr 29, 1891; May 1, 1891; Lots 29-
32, Block 38 town of Norman, OT;
Warranty Deed.

1:83   Bondurant, J.D. and Myrah Gray
(husband & wife) to Beishause,
Frank; Apr 17, 1891; May 1, 1891;
Lots 12 & 13 & 31 & 32 Block 47,
& Lot 8 & 9 Blk 57, & Lots 20-32
Blk 81, Lots 1-13 Blk 88 town of
Lexington, OT; Bondurants of
Louisville, Kentucky; Warranty
Deed.

1:84   Emmons, J.B. & Mollie C. (his wife)
to Beaublossom, Jacob; Apr 20,
1891; May 1, 1891; Lots 30-34, Blk

87, city of Norman, OT; Warranty
Deed.

1:85   Elkins, James (single man) to Elkins,
       George; Apr 25, 1891; May 1, 1891;
       Lot 21, Blk 41, town of Lexington,
       OT; Warranty Deed.

1:86   Lacy, J.D. & M.S. (his wife) &
       Lacy, Nancy D. (single woman) to
       Bessent, C.H.; Apr 24, 1891; May 1,
       1891; Lots 10 & 11, Blk 32, village
       of Norman, OT; J.D. Lacy cannot
       write; Warranty Deed; Harris, S.H.
       & McGinley, M.

1:87   Wiesehann, Gerhard W. to Smith,
       George; Apr 22, 1891; May 1, 1891;
       Lots 26-28 Blk 38, town of Norman,
       OT; Warranty Deed.

1:88   Brady, Frank to Wiesehann, Gerhard
       W.; Apr 22, 1891; May 7, 1891;
       Lots 13-16, Blk 2, town of Norman,
       OT; Warranty Deed.

1:89   Hunter, A.T. (unmarried) to Haddix,
       Martha F.; May 2, 1891; May 7,

1891; Lots 17 & 18 Blk 4, Norman,
OT; Warranty Deed.

1:90   Fenelon, Mary (widow) to Hunter,
A.T.; May 2, 1891; May 9,1891;
Lots 15 & 16 Blk 32, Norman, OT;
John H. Fenelon, attorney for Mary
Fenelon; Warranty Deed.

1:91   White, T.J. & D.V. (his wife) to
Switzer, E.M;. May 2, 1891; May 9,
1891; Lots 1-3, Blk 88, town of
Norman, OT; Warranty Deed.

1:92   Klinglesmith, J.W. & Sarah (his
wife) to Hay, Daniel; May 4, 1891;
May 9, 1891; Lots 9-16 & 26-30,
Blk 45, Noble, OT; Warranty Deed.

1:93   Westbrook, C.H. & Maria (his wife)
to Shannon, J.R.; May 5, 1891; May
11, 1891; Lots 7-9, Blk 32, Norman,
OT; Power of attorney recorded
Book 1, page 4; Warranty Deed;
E.M. Westbrook, attorney in fact.

1:94   Helm, Elmer C. (single man) to
Horn, William H.; May 5, 1891;

May 14, 1891; SW4 Sec 35 T11N
R3W; Helm from Canadian County,
OT; Horn from Oklahoma County,
OT; Warranty Deed; Lindsey, J.S.

1:95   Horn, William H. to Burt, John A.;
May 5, 1891; May 14, 1891;
SW4 Sec 35 T11N R3W; Warranty
Deed; Elder, J.H.

1:96   Trustees of township of Lexington:
Leavy, Samuel; Joyce, Robert; &
Hay, Daniel; Certificate #84; Mar 13,
1891; May 12, 1891; S2 SW4 Sec. 5
& SE4 SE4 Sec 6 & NE4 NE4 Sec
7 T6N R1W.

1:97   Larsh, D.L. & Nellie (his wife) to
Poole, W.B.;   Apr 3, 1891; May 12,
1891; Lots 18-20 Blk 70, Norman,
OT in D.L. Larsh #1 addition;
Warranty Deed; Moore, S.M.

1:98   Wallace, W.T. & M.E. (his wife) to
Poole, W.B.; Apr 3, 1891; May 12,
1891; Lots 17-19, Blk 70, Waggoner
1st Addition, Norman, OT ;
Warranty Deed.

17

1:99   Hoover, M.D. (unmarried man) to
       Wallace, Wiley T.; May 5, 1891;
       May 13, 1891; Lots 2-5, Blk 70,
       Norman, OT; Warranty Deed.

1:100 Poole, W.B. (unmarried man) to
       Bessent, C.H.; May 7, 1891; May 13,
       1891; Lots 17-20, Blk 70, Larsh &
       Waggoner 1st Additions of the city of
       Norman, OT; Warranty Deed;
       Grigsby, J.E. & Bellamy, George.

1:101 Flood, John H. & Martha J. (his wife)
       to Martin, W.D.; May 6, 1891; May
       13, 1891; Lots 28-30, Blk 74,
       Norman, OT; Warranty Deed.

1:102 Boggs, B.L. to Martin, W.D.; May 9,
       1891; May 14, 1891; Lots 25-27 Blk
       74, Norman, OT; Warranty Deed.

1:103 Foster, T.E. to Bonstead, R.D.;
       May 9, 1891; May 14, 1891;
       half interest Lots 1 & 2, Blk 56,
       Lexington, OT; Warranty Deed;
       Buler, B.F.

1:104 Clayton, Frank E. & Agnes M. (his

wife) to Seawell, W.H.; Mar 25,
1891; May 14, 1891; Lot 27, Blk 5,
Norman, OT; Warranty Deed;
Morrison, Jesse S.

1:105   Wallace, Wiley T. & M.E. (his wife)
        to Elliott, T.B.; May 7, 1891; May
        15, 1891; Lot 28, Blk 86, Waggoner
        Addition, Norman, OT, Warranty
        Deed.

1:106   Hoovers, S.C. & M.D. (unmarried
        persons) to Hendricks, T.W.; May
        18, 1891; May 22, 1891; Lots 1-11
        Blk 83 & 15-16 Blk 72, Norman,
        OT; Warranty Deed.

1:107   Colley, George H. & Josie M. (his
        wife) to Downing, Hiram; May 21,
        1891; May 21, 1891; Lots 8-15, Blk
        3, Colley 2nd Addition to City of
        Norman, OT; Warranty Deed;
        Bellamy, William H.

1:108   Albright, James T. & R.E. (his wife)
        to Carter, Julia A.; May 21, 1891;
        May 22, 1891; Lot 22, Blk 15,
        Norman, OT; Warranty Deed;

Bellamy, William H.

1:109 Williams, John B. & Annie E. (his
wife) to Minnear, Garrett; May 22,
1891; May 23, 1891; SW4 Sec 11
T9N R3W; Warranty Deed; Belden,
Z. & Robertson, Samuel.

1:110 Bessent, C.H. & Jennie E. (his wife)
to Merkle, Sarah C.; May 22, 1891;
May 22, 1891; Lots 10 & 11, Blk 32
Norman, OT; Warranty Deed;
Bellamy, William H.

1:111 Caldwell, T.O. & B.I. (his wife) to
Dickerson, J.J.; April 6, 1891;May
23, 1891; Lot 16, Blk 55 in
Lexington, OT; Caldwell's from
Grayson Co., Texas; Warranty Deed;
Coffin, A.H.

1:112 Jackson, John M. & Minnie (his wife)
to McGee, J.D.; May 8, 1891; May
18, 1891; Lots 6 to 9 , Blk 73 &
Lots 15 & 16 in Blk 65 & Lots 12 to
16 in Blk 83, Norman, OT; Jackson's
from Waldo, Columbia County,
Arkansas; Warranty Deed; Pace,C.H.

20

1:114 Carr, W.H. to Dickerson, James J.;
Apr 29, 1891; May 23, 1891; Lots
24 Blk 66 S2 of SW4 of Lexington,
OT; Sec 5 T6N R1W; Carr from
Lamar Co, Texas; Warranty Deed;
Kavanaugh, W.B., County Clerk of
Lamar County, Texas.

1:115 Gaylord, John B. & Ella R. (his wife)
to Burroge, J.E.;. Apr 22, 1891; May
23, 1891; Lots 27 & 28 Blk 24
Norman, OT; Ella Gaylord in Eaton
Co., Michigan; Warranty Deed;
Ross, A.T.

1:116 Bell, James to Carter, Julia A..;
Nov 1, 1890; May 23, 1891; Lots 20
& 21 in Blk 15 Norman, OT; Bell
from Purcell, IT; Indenture.

1:117 White, Kate R. & Martin M. (her
husband) to Merkle, Sarah E.; May
26, 1891; May 26,1891; Lot 10 & 11
Blk 33, Norman, OT; Warranty
Deed; Cook, Thomas R.

1:118 Curtice, Solon & Eve Cole (his wife)
to Remington, J.M.; May 18, 1891;

May 23, 1891; Lot 20 Blk 42 town
of Lexington, OT;   Indenture.

1:119 Colley, George H. & Josie M. (his
wife) to Whitley, Viola; May 28,
1891; May 28, 1891; Lot 4, Blk 4 in
Colley First Addition in Norman,
OT; Warranty Deed.

1:120 Gordon, S.W. & Addie (his wife) to
McGinley, F.J.; May 13, 1891; May
28, 1891; NW4 of SE4 Sec 29
T9N R2W; 5.35 acres; Addie Gordon
signed in Polk County, Missouri;
Warranty Deed.

1:122 Colley, George H. & Josie M. (his
wife) to Denney, Mrs. S.C.; May
28, 1891; May 29, 1891; incomplete
legal description; Warranty Deed;
Bellamy, William H. & Crawford,
Will C.

1:123 Kolley, Joseph A. & Mattie E. (his
wife) to Briggs, L.L. & Capshaw,
M.T.J.; May 28, 1891; May 29,
1891; Lot 6, Blk 6, Norman, OT;
Warranty Deed.

1:124   Beale, Robert W. (single man) to
        Beale, Andrew J.; May 27, 1891;
        June 2, 1891; NW4 Sec 15 T10N
        R3W; Andrew J. Beale of Oklahoma
        County, OT; Warranty Deed.

1:125   Bitsche, Edward to Bitsche, Emily;
        June 4, 1891; June 5, 1891; Lot 3 &
        4 and S2 NW4 Sec 4 T6N R1W;
        Warranty Deed.

1:126   Westbrook, E.M. (single person) to
        Miller, J.K.; June 2, 1891; June 15,
        1891; Lots 17-21, Block 10,
        Norman, OT; W.A. Wood.

1:127   Ferguson, William H. (single person)
        to McMahon, John; May 19, 1891;
        June 15, 1891; SE4 NW4 Sec 31
        T9N R2W; Warranty Deed; T.R.
        Waggoner.

1:128   Shannon, J.R. (single) to Hunter,
        A.T.; June 3, 1891; June 3, 1891;
        Lots 7-9, Block 32, & 31-21, Block
        15 Norman, OT; Shannon is from
        Purcell, IT; Warranty Deed.

1:129 Criswell, John R. & Mollie E. (his
       wife) to Boston, James; May 29,
       1891; June 15, 1891; Lots 9-10
       Block 38 Norman, OT; Mollie
       Criswell signed in Johnson Co.,
       Texas; Warranty Deed.

1:130 Conrad, James W. & Lee O. (wife) to
       Essex, John; May 11, 1891; June 15,
       1891; Lots 4-7 Block 20 Norman,
       OT; Warranty Deed.

1:131 Gordon, S.W. & Addie (wife) to
       Briggs, L.L.; June 5, 1891; June 17,
       1891; 8 acres; Sec 29 T9N R2W;
       Addie Gordon signed in Polk
       County, Missouri; Warranty Deed.

1:133 Hendricks, T.W. & Victoria (wife) to
       Moore, J.T.; June 15, 1891; June 15,
       1891; Lots 23-24, Block 67,
       Norman, OT; Warranty Deed.

1:134 Wallace, W.T. & M.E. (wife) to
       LeGors, Rufus; June 15, 1891; June
       17, 1891; Lots 17-23, Block 86,
       Waggoner's 1st Addition of
       Norman, OT; Grantee name could be

LeFore; Warranty Deed.

1:135   McGinley, Frank (single man) to
Mayfield, Mrs. Sarah; June 16, 1891;
June 17, 1891; Lots 4-5, Block 19,
Norman, OT; Warranty Deed; Wm.
H. Bellamy & Hugh Jones.

1:136   Gordon, S.W. & Addie (his wife) to
Aniol, Robert & Synnott, Ellen;
June 8, 1891; June 18, 1891;
1/3 interest in SE4 of Sec 29 T9N
R2W; 39.65 acres; Addie Gordon
signed in Polk County, Missouri;
Warranty Deed.

1:138   Westbrook, C.H. to Marr, N.; June
16, 1891; June 17, 1891; Lots 22-32
Blk 82 in Norman, OT; E.M.
Westbrook, attorney in fact, single
person; Warranty Deed.

1:139   Westbrook, E.M. to   Marr, N.;
June 16, 1891; June 17, 1891; Lots
20-22 Blk 64 in Norman, OT; E.M.
Westbrook is a single person;
Warranty Deed.

1:140 Wallace, W.T. & M.E. (his wife) to
Elliott, T.B.; June 16, 1891; June 17,
1891; Lots 25-27 Blk 86 in
Waggoner's Addition of Norman,
OT; Warranty Deed.

1:141 Andrew, Cassius W. (single) to
Hay, Daniel; June 22, 1891; June 22,
1891; Lot 1-1`6 Blk 63 Noble, OT;
Andrew from Noble, OT; Warranty
Deed; Wm. H. Bellamy.

1:142 Gordon, S.W. & Addie (his wife) to
Runyan, M.C.; June 5, 1891; June
17, 1891; part of the SE4 containing
2 acres Sec 29 T9N R 2W; Addie
Gordon signed in Polk County,
Missouri; Warranty Deed.

1:144 Frazey, George W. & Emily F. (his
wife) to Gibbs, George W.; June 23,
1891; June 23, 1891; N2 NW4 Sec
27 T9N R1W; 80 acres, was their
homestead; Warranty Deed.

1:145 Hendricks, T.W. & Victoria (his
wife) to Adkins, Pryor; June 20,
1891; June 20, 1891; Lots 30 Blk

71 Norman, OT; Quit Claim Deed.

1:146 Hope, Sarah B. (widow) to Mayfield, Sarah; June 22, 1891; June 22, 1891; Lots 24 & 25 Blk 16 Norman, OT; Hope from Purcell, IT; Warranty Deed; Hope, R.S.

1:147 Hendricks, T.W. & Victoria (his wife) to Williams, John B.; June 25, 1891; June 26, 1891; Lots 5 & 13 - 17 in Blk 87 in Norman, OT; Warranty Deed.

1:148 Boyle, J.P. as receiver for Ragsdale, J.M. & McClain, C.R. & Corrette, Ed dba Commercial Bank to Marquart, D.W.; June 19, 1891; June 23, 1891; Lot 16 Blk 5 Norman, OT; J.P. Boyle appointed receiver by court; Receivers Deed.

1:150 Marquart, D.W. & M.E. (his wife) to Citizen's Bank of Norman, OT; June 23, 1891; June 23, 1891; Lot 16 Blk 5 Norman, OT; Quit Claim Deed.

1:151   Grigsby, J.E. to Grigsby, Elizabeth J.
(his wife); July 20, 1891; July 22,
1891; Lot 3 Blk 5 Norman, OT;
Land previously owned by J.D.
Grigsby; Warranty Deed.

1:152   Cole, Sydney S. & Pauline A. (his
wife) to Peery, E.H.; July 11, 1891;
July 25, 1891; SE4 Sec20 T4W
R10N; Warranty Deed; Davis, R.A.
& Kennedy, James.

1:153   Colley, George H. to Nix, W.R.;
Jan 12, 1891; Aug 1, 1891; Lots 1-3
Blk 3 Colley's First Addition to
Norman, OT; Josie M. Colley
relinquished dower as wife; Warranty
Deed.

1:154   Bondurant, J.D. & Myrah Gray
Bondurant (his wife) to Benshouse,
Frank; July 22, 1891; July 31, 1891;
Lots 12-18 Blk 26; Lots 9-16 Blk 21;
Lots 1-3 in Blk 44 in Lexington, OT;
All from Louisville, Kentucky;
Warranty Deed.

1:155   Jennison, W.R. & A.B. (his wife) to

Jennison Bros. & Co.; July 30, 1891;
July 31, 1891; All of Blk 69 Lots 1-7
in Norman, OT; Quit Claim Deed;
Davis, Robert A.

1:156 Jennison, Mrs. Anna E. to Jennisson,
William B. and Harry; Aug 20, 1890;
Aug 24, 1891; Lot 10-12 in Blk 69
& Lots 1-7 in Blk 69 in Norman,
OT; Anna is in Chicago, Cook Co,
Illinois; Quit Claim Deed.

1:158 Moore, Seth M. & Martha K. (his
wife) to University of Oklahoma;
July 8, 1891; Aug 26, 1891;W2 NE4
& E2 NW4 SE4 Sec 31 T2W R9N
to establish the University of
Oklahoma; Warranty Deed.

1:159 Avriett, James & Annie (his wife) to
Jones, Paul; Aug 26, 1891; Sept. 2,
1891; ½ interest in Lot 5 Blk 22 in
Norman, OT; Parties of Henderson
Co., Texas; Warranty Deed; J.B.
Bishop, Allie Brock.

1:160 Blake, Tyler & Mary E. (his wife) &
Blake, George and his wife, Ella to

York, C.F.; Aug 22, 1891; Sept 5, 1891; Lots 32, 30 & 29 Blk 13 in Norman, OT; York from Collin Co., Texas; Blake homestead; Warranty Deed; T.E. Berry.

1:161 Curtice, Solon & Eva M. (his wife) to Remington, John M.; July 1, 1891; Sept 7, 1891; Lots 21-24 Blk 16 in Lexington, OT, ½ interest; Warranty Deed; E.J. Keller.

1:162 Remington, John M.. & Lena (his wife) to Curtice, Solon; July 1, 1891; Sept 7, 1891; Lots 29-32 Blk 16 in Lexington, OT, ½ interest; Warranty Deed; E.J. Keller & G.P. Johnston.

1:163 Carlock, Andrew M. & Luella (his wife) to Studer, Edward; Sept 21, 1891; Sept 22, 1891; NW4 Sec 8 T3W R10N; name maybe Sluder; Warranty Deed; S.J. Cullom.

1:164 Major, Olive A. & Louie O. (husband & wife) to Straka, Mary; Sept 15, 1891; Sept 19, 1891; NW4 Sec 32

T3W R11N; name may be Clive not
Olive; Warranty Deed; D.C. Lewis.

1:165 Cozart, James W. & Monice J. (his
wife) to Starling, J.A. & M.T. (his
wife); Sept 21, 1891; Sept 21, 1891;
Lots 17 - 22 Blk 55 in Norman, OT;
Quit Claim Deed.

1:166 Kramer, L.F. (single man) to
Dollmeier. Mike & Billen, Peter;
Sept 19, 1891; Sept 30, 1891; Lots
3, 4 & S2 NW4 Sec 5 T3W R10 N;
Warranty Deed; L.A. Gilbert.

1:167 Inbody, Ephraim & Mindia (his wife)
to Inbody, Samuel (his brother);
Oct 14, 1891; Oct 14, 1891;W2 SW4
Sec 22 T82N R7W in Linn Co.,
Iowa; heirs at law of Samuel Inbody,
dec'd 1/7 interest.

1:168 Dear, William E. (single man) to
Jameson, B.F.; Oct 2, 1891; Oct 19,
1891; NE4 Sec 23 T4W R10N; Dear
from Oklahoma Co., OT; Warranty
Deed; S.A. Steward.

31

1:169   Bonneau, Salyone & Elizabeth (his
        wife) to Forehand, H.L.; Sept 16,
        1891; Oct 5, 1891; Lot 11 Blk 55 in
        Lexington, OT; Warranty Deed.

1:170   Wallace, W.T. & M.E. (his wife) to
        Graham, Rosa A.; Oct 10, 1891; Oct
        10, 1891; Lots 21-23 Blk 11 in T.R.
        Waggoner's 1st Addition to Norman,
        OT;   Warranty Deed.

1:171   Larsh, Delbert L. & Nellie (his wife)
        to Graham, Rosa A.; Oct 10, 1891;
        Oct 13, 1891; Lots 21-23 Blk 11 in
        D.L. Larsh 1st Addition to Norman,
        OT; Warranty Deed; S.M. Moore.

1:172   Smith, Jennie B. & Percy R. (her
        husband) to Hocker, James W.;
        Oct 12, 1891; Nov 4, 1891; Lots 23-
        27 Blk 26 in Lexington, OT; Smiths
        from Lexington, OT.

1:173   Hembree, Charles C. & Rosa (his
        wife) to Munn, John A.; Mar 17,
        1891; Nov 4, 1891; Lot 22 Blk 71 in
        Norman, OT; Hembrees from New
        York Co., N Y; Rosa signed in Knox

Co., Ohio; Warranty Deed; William
Grier & Varian Banks.

1:174 Schmuck, V.E. & Elizabeth (his wife)
to Schottenkirk, Jay; Mar 14, 1891;
NE4 Sec 18 T2W R9N; All parties
from Woodford Co., Illinois;
Warranty Deed.

1:175 McCarty, L. to McCarty, Jennie;
Dec 19, 1890; Lots 12-14 Blk 69
D.L. Larsh 1st Addition to Norman,
OT; L. McCarty from Collin Co.,
Texas; Warranty Deed.

1:176 Beeler, George R. & Georgie (his
wife) to Gillock, William; Feb 9,
1891; Dec 1, 1891; Lots 29-30 Blk
22 in Norman, OT.

1:177 Hamilton, J.C. & Mary C. (his wife)
to Ward, Harry; Nov 26, 1891; Nov
26, 1891; Lots 17 & 18 in Blk 8 in
Norman, OT; Warranty Deed;
Jay Thompson.

1:178 Lappin, James & Mary C. (his wife)
to Hawk, A.D.; Jul 16, 1891; Dec 3,

1891; Lots 7& 8 Blk 55 in
Lexington, OT; Hawk from Purcell,
IT; Lappin from Lexington, OT;
Warranty Deed.

1:179   Hawk, Alfred D. & Lucy W. (his
        wife) to Hocker, Walter E.; Dec 1,
        1891; Dec 3, 1891; Lots 7 & 8 Blk
        55 & Lot 16 Blk 54 in Lexington,
        OT; Hawk's from Purcell, IT; release
        in Misc. Book 3 page 292; Vendor's
        lien.

1:180   Carleton, Henry M. (single man) to
        Southern Kansas Railway Co.;
        Nov 3, 1891; NW4 Sec 27 T 2W
        R8N; Warranty Deed.

1:182   McKinley, J.F. & Arabella (his wife)
        to Carter, Frederick; Dec 3, 1891;
        Lot 10 Blk 22 in Norman, OT;
        Warranty Deed.

1:183   Streeter, Charles M. & Hattie (his
        wife) to Cobb, John P.; Dec 15,
        1891; Lot 5, Blk 14, Norman, OT;
        Streeter from Sedgwick Co.,
        Kansas; Warranty Deed.

1:184   Cunningham, Con to Cunningham,
        M.; Oct 21, 1891; SE4 Sec10 T 9N
        R3W; Cunningham from Dawson,
        Navarro Co., Texas; Warranty Deed.

1:185   Haas, R.P. to Ducas, Cezar; Dec 4,
        1891; Lots 25, Blk 5, Lexington,
        OT; Warranty Deed; J. Thompson.

1:186   Bowling, C.G. & Alice (his wife) to
        Dessent, C.H., as agent for J.M.
        Curtice; Dec 5, 1891; Dec19, 1891;
        W2 NW4 NE4 Sec 29 T9N R2W;
        Title came by Land Cert. #145,
        Book 1; Warranty Deed.

1:187   Owens, S.B. & Etta (his wife) to
        Sauls, W.D.; Dec 19, 1891; Dec 28,
        1891; Part of NE4 Sec 29 T9N R2W
        Blk B in Owens Addition; Warranty
        Deed.

1:188   Brown, Samuel H. & Lina (his wife)
        to Newby, Lewis; Dec 22, 1891;
        Dec 23, 1891; SE4 Sec2 T10N
        R3W; Newby from Oklahoma Co.,
        OT; Warranty Deed; John T. Welch
        & J.N. White.

1:189 Newby, Lewis & Catharine (his wife)
to Brown, Samuel H. & Lina (his
wife); Dec 29, 1891; Dec 30, 1891;
SE4 Sec 2 T10N R3W; Warranty
Deed; Francis A. McKennon & W.L.
McKennon.

1:190 Curtice, J.M. (single man) to Arnold,
Wootson & Mary; Nov 30, 1891; Jan
28, 1892; Lots 3-5 and SE4 NE4 Sec
6 T10N R2W; Curtice signed in
Kings Co., NY; Warranty Deed.

1:191 Anderson, W.A. & E.L. (his wife) to
Renfrow, W.C.; Dessent, C.H.;
Reynolds, George T.; Poole, W.B.;
Richardson, T.M.; Caruthers, F.; dba
Norman State Bank; Jan 15, 1892;
Jan 30, 1892; Lots 16, Blk 6,
Norman, OT; Warranty Deed.

1:192 Carlock, James A. & C.M. (his wife)
to Fisher, A.W.; Oct 15, 1891; Feb
2, 1892; Lot 26-28 Blk 11, Norman,
OT; Carlocks in Dade Co., Missouri;
Quit Claim Deed.

1:193 Stewart, Sarah E. & Henry W. (her

husband) to Carr, Eva; Dec 26,1891;
Feb 2, 1892; Lots 26, Blk 32,
Lexington, OT; Warranty Deed.

1:194 Williams, J.B. & Annie E. (his wife)
to Ellidge, W.N.; Apr 15, 1891; Feb
2, 1892; Lots #1 and A, B, & C, Blk
70, Norman, OT; Warranty Deed.

1:195 Whitehead, C. to Porta, W.L.; Feb 8,
1892; Lot 28 & 29, Blk 7, Norman,
OT; All parties in Cook Co., Texas;
Warranty Deed.

1:196 Alley, John W. & Lucinda (his wife)
to Hill, John D.; Feb 4, 1892; Feb 16,
1892; Lots 2-4 Sec 31 T7N R1W;
Hill is from Parker Co., Texas;
Warranty Deed; J. Thompson.

1:197 Judkins, George & Frances (his wife)
to Jennings, Lyndal C.; Nov 20,
1891; Lots 3 & 4 and the E2 SW4
Sec 18 T7N R1W; Jennings from
Pontotoc Co., Chickasaw Nation;
Warranty Deed; George W. Miller.

1:199 Johnson, E.B. & W.H. (her husband)

to Dorrance, Mary E.; Feb 3, 1892;
Lots 5 & 6, Blk 3, Norman, OT;
Warranty Deed.

1:200 Cornell, Smith P. & Ella (his wife)
to Cornell, Joshand? (wife of Elijah
M.) Feb 4, 1892; Lots 1-12 & 17-26
& 28-32, Blk 33, Noble, OT; Sellers
from Logan Co., OT; buyers from
from Navarro Co., Texas; Warranty
Deed.

1:202 Johnson, T.J. & M.F. (his wife) to
Keener, James L.; Jan 29, 1892;
Lot 2 Blk 2, Johnson Claim; part of
SW4 Sec 27 T9N R2W; Keener
from Wynnewood, IT.;Warranty
Deed.

1:204 U.S. government, President Benjamin
Harrison to Trustees of Lexington,
OT; Bish, James M.;Larsh, Delbert
L.; Leavy, Samuel T.; Jan 25, 1892;
Feb 27, 1892; Town site of
Lexington, OT; SW4 SE4 Sec 6
T6N   R1N; Cert. #355.

1:206 U.S. government, President Benjamin

Harrison to Trustees of Lexington,
OT; Bish, James M.; Larsh, Delbert
L.; Leavy, Samuel T.; Jan 25, 1892;
Feb 27, 1892; Town site of Norman,
OT; E2 SW4 Sec 29 T9N R2W;
Cert. #353.

1:208 Dye, Thomas & Loretta L. (his wife)
to Leigh, Edward; Feb 10, 1892; Feb
11, 1892; S2 NE4 & Lots 1 & 2
Sec 5 T10N R4W; Warranty Deed;
John R. Furlong.

1:209 Krahl, G.N. & P.D. (his wife) to
Krahl, W.D.; Jan 9, 1892; Feb 19,
1892; Lots 3 & 4, Blk 52, Norman,
OT; Sellers are in Bedford, Taylor
Co., Iowa; Warranty Deed; J.H.
Fitch & Chas. V. Dripes.

1:210 Averyt, A.N. & Meddia C. (his wife)
to Conley, A.J.; Nov 28, 1891; Feb
20, 1892; Lots 17-20 Blk 21
Norman, OT.

1:211 Owens, S.B. & Etta (his wife) to
Cleveland County, OT; Mar 7,
1892; For the use of hyways 30 feet

39

wide; NE4 Sec 29 T9N R2W;
Warranty Deed.

1:213 McKinley, J.F. & Arabella (his wife)
to Carter, Frederick; Feb 13, 1892;
Paid off note; Indenture.

1:214 McKinley, J.F. & Bell (his wife) to
Roberts, Nace G.; Oct 21, 1891; Feb
22, 1892; Lots 24-26 Blk 35
Norman, OT; Warranty Deed.

1:216 Redmen, Curthey S. & Susie (his
wife) to Blackburn, W.P.; Feb 20,
1892; Feb 23, 1892; SE4 Sec 5
T10N R4W; Cowley Co., Kansas
where Susie Redman was signing;
Warranty Deed; Hillman, Hugh H. &
R.A. Gilmer.

1:218 Little, Woodward & Mary C. (his
wife) to Lindenour, Henry; Feb 13,
1892; E2 NW4 Sec 10 T6N R1W;
Warranty Deed; Ben Murphy, B.B.
Blakeney.

1:220 Robinson, Ira to School District #4
Cleveland Co., OT; Jan 20, 1891;

1 acre NW4 Sec 25 T10N R2W.

1:221 Loofbourraw, J.S. to Loofbourraw,
D.B.; Mar 11, 1892; Mar 12, 1892;
Lots 7, 8 25, & 26 Blk 37 Lexington,
OT; Loofbourraw, D.B. of Wilson
Co., Kansas; Warranty Deed; T.B.
Dirk.

1:223 Judkins, George & Sarah (his wife)
to Brown, Helen L.; Apr 11, 1891;
SW4 Sec 18 T7N R1W; See Misc.
Book 2 page 31; Indenture; James
M. Goodin.

1:225 Graves, H.C. & W.C. to Perry,
W.C.; Mar 14, 1892; Selling 1/3
interest in Graves Bros. partnership
to pay notes; Indenture; George
Symer, J.T. Rutherford.

1:229 Little, Woodward & Mary C. (his
wife) to Lindemann, Henry; Feb 17,
1892; Feb 17, 1892; E2 NW4 Sec10
T6N R1W; Warranty Deed;
Ben Murphy & B.B. Blakeney.

1:230 Stewart, Sarah E. & Henry W. (her

husband) to Dent, Horace F.; Apr 6,
1892; Apr 8, 1892; Lot 12 Blk 58 in
Lexington, OT; Dent from Jackson
Co., Missouri; Warranty Deed;
Neil Smith.

1:231   Carr, W.H. & Eva A. (his wife) to
Elkins, George; Mar 23, 1892; Apr
5, 1892; Lots 1-6, 27-32, Blk 31 &
Lots 21-23 Blk; Warranty Deed;
James W. Hocken.

1:232   Colley, George H. & Josie M. (his
wife) to Turk, Herman; Mar 22,
1892; Mar 23, 1892; Lots 3-6 Blk 4
Colley's 2nd Addition in Norman,
OT; Warranty Deed.

1:233   Elkins, Mattie B. & Charles (her
husband) to Hocken, Walter E.;
Mar 23, 1892; Mar 24, 1892; Lots 20
Blk 42 in Lexington, OT; Hocken
from Sacred Heart, OT; H. W.
Stewart.

1:234   Arthur, James W. & Susan M. (his
wife) to Minor, D.A.; Apr 7, 1892;
Apr 9, 1892; Lot 9, 10 Blk 3 Colley's

1ˢᵗ Addition in Norman, OT;
Arthur's from Logan Co., OT;
Warranty Deed; Fred E. Miller.

1:235   Boling, C.G. & Alice (his wife) to
Trustees of Methodist Church South,
A.W. Averyh, J.M. Chastaine, J.P.
Jackson, J.E. Turner, W.H. Seawell;
Apr 4, 1891; Apr 15, 1892; NE4 Sec
29 T9N R2W 10 acres for Oklahoma
District High School of the
Methodist Church South; Warranty
Deed.

1:237   Adams, Edward L. to Grisby, J.E.;
Jan 7, 1892; Apr 1, 1892; Lot 22-28,
Blk 10, Norman, OT; Warranty
Deed.

1:238   Jackson, J.M. & Minnie (his wife) to
McGee, J.D.; Feb 27, 1892; Apr
1892; Lot 6-9, Blk 73, & Lot 12-16,
Blk 83, Norman, OT; Deed made in
Columbia Co., Arkansas; Warranty
Deed.

1:239   Smith, Sallie (Belcher) & J.B. (her
husband) to Carder, Frederick;

43

Apr 9, 1892; Apr 14, 1892; SE4
Sec 8 T8N R2W; Smiths' of
Ardmore, Chickasaw Nation, OT;
Warranty Deed.

1:240   Owens, S.B. & Etta (his wife) to
Hall, Mrs. S.E.; Apr 5, 1892; Apr 5,
1892; 4 acres in NE4 Sec 29 T9N
R2W; Mrs. Hall from Sherman,
Texas; Warranty Deed.

1:241   Anderson, W.A. & E.S. (his wife) to
Wingate, W.W.; Apr 1892; Apr 21,
1892; Lot 3-5, Blk 84, Norman, OT;
Warranty Deed; A.N. Elvington &
O.D. Wimberly.

1:243   Starkey, John & Martha A. (his wife)
to Starkey, Jos./Joe Feb 3, 1892; Apr
29, 1892; Lots 1-33, Blk 30,
Lexington, OT; Warranty Deed;
H.T. Bowie.

1:244   Starkey, John & Martha A. (his wife)
to Starkey, Joe; Feb 3, 1892; Apr 29,
1892; Lot 29, Blk 42, in ?? and
house and fixtures; Warranty Deed;
H.T. Bowie.

1:245 Richardson, J.I. & Nannie (his wife)
to Murchison, D.R.; Apr 21, 1892;
May 3, 1892; Lot 25-32, Blk 22,
Waggoner's 1st Addition to Norman,
OT; Richardsons from Henderson
Co., Texas; Warranty Deed.

1:246 Walker, John I. (single man) to
Erwin, Oliver T.; Apr 9, 1892; May
2, 1892; Lots 10-12 & 21-23, Blk
54, Norman, OT; Walker from
Oklahoma Co., OT; Warranty Deed.

1:247 Oklahoma Lumber Co. by W.L. &
Ella Choate, W.P. & Emma Seawell,
J.E. & Eddie Waggoner (married
couples), and O.H. Benton (single
man) to Edwards, L.J.; Mar 29,
1892; Apr 28, 1892; Lot 1-4, Blk 6,
Norman, OT; Seawells reside in
Jackson Co., Missouri; Waggoners
from Lafayette Co., Missouri;
Warranty Deed.

1:249 Knapp, A.J. & A.E. (his wife) to
T.M. Richardson Lumber Co.;
Mar 29, 1892; Apr 11, 1892; Lot 25,
Blk 42, Lexington, OT; Warranty

Deed; Stuart, S.W.

1:250   Johnson, T.J. & M.F. (his wife) to
        Williams, Mrs. E.H.; Jan 26, 1892;
        May 2, 1892; Lot 2, Blk 1, T.J.
        Johnson claim, Norman, OT;
        Warranty Deed.

1:252   Johnson, T.J. & M.F. (his wife) to
        Cameron, E.D.; Jan 26, 1892; May
        1892; 1 acres in SW4 Sec 21 T9N
        R2W; Warranty Deed.

1:254   Renfrow, W.C. & Jannie B. (his wife)
        to Jones, J.A.; May 2, 1892; May 10,
        1892; Lot 2, Blk 14, Norman, OT;
        Warranty Deed; W.S. Riggins &
        C.H. Bessent.

1:255   Arnold, Wootson H. & Mary S. (his
        wife) to Gysett, John; May 12, 1892;
        May 12, 1892; Lot 3-5, SE4 NW4
        Sec 6 T10N R2W; All parties from
        Oklahoma Co., OT; Warranty Deed.

1:256   James, James M. & Emily (his wife)
        to Harriss, W.J.; May 18, 1892; May
        18, 1892; 160 acres in NW4 Sec 21

T8N R1W; Warranty Deed.

1:257 Thomsen, G. & Sophia (his wife) to
Arnold, W.H.; May 12, 1892; May
16, 1892; 157+ acres in Lot 3-5, SE4
NW4 Sec 6 T10N R2W; Quit
Claim deed.

1:258 McDonald, W.R. & Mary G. (his
wife) to Trustees of M.E. Church;
Feb 25, 1892; May 12, 1892; SW4
Sec 17 T7N R1W; Property to be
used as a place of worship or revert
to seller; Quit Claim Deed; Reuben
Haas.

1:260 Estate of James Calvert, dec'd;
Parmelia Calvert, adx and guardian
of Joseph & Mable Calvert of
Oklahoma Co., OT to Courtney, J.G.
of Oklahoma Co., OT; May 13,
1892; May 16, 1892; Lot 17 Blk 32
in Norman, OT; Indenture.

1:262 Remington, J.M. & Lena (his wife) to
Elkin, Mattie B.; Jan 28, 1892; Jan
28, 1892; Lexington, OT Lot 20 Blk
42 aka as Remington Drug Store

Property; Remington's signed in Tecumseh, Co., "B", OT; Warranty Deed; James W. Hocker, Chickasaw Nation.

1:263   Hann, J.P.N. & Vastie to Bible, Solen A.; May 27, 1892; May 27, 1892; Lots 9 & 10 Blk 29 in Norman, OT; Hann homestead; Warranty Deed.

1:264   Jones, Hughbert (single man) to Jones, J.A.; May 10, 1892; May 15, 1892; Part of NE4, contains 57.77 acres Sec 31 T2W R9N; Warranty Deed; George B. House & Syker, S.L.

1:265   Bible, Solen A. (single man) to Hann, J.P.N.; May 27, 1892; May 27, 1892; Lots # 12 & 13 Blk 29 in Norman, OT; Warranty Deed.

1:266   Fox, F.M. & S.J. (his wife) from Pontotoc Co., Chickasaw Nation, IT to Martin, West; May 27, 1892; May 28, 1892; Lots 19 & 20 in Blk 33 in Norman, OT; Warranty Deed;

H.B. Campbell.

1:267 Terry, J.W. & Katie (his wife) to
Felkner, C.H. from Dallas Co.,
Texas; Nov 15, 1890; May 1892;
Lots 20-23 Blk 20 in Norman, OT;
Warranty Deed; S.M. Moore.

1:268 Felkner, C.H. & P.E. (his wife) from
Dallas, Texas to Rogers, William
from Dallas Co., Texas; May 26,
1892; Lots 20-23 Blk 20 in
Norman, OT; Warranty Deed.

1:269 Courtney, James G. & Lillie G. (his
wife) from Oklahoma Co., OT to
Kramer, L.F.; Jun 1, 1892; Jun 1,
1892; Lot 17 Blk 32 in Norman, OT;
Warranty Deed.

1:270 Carr, W.H. to Black, Richard;
Jun 3, 1892; Jun 3, 1892; Carr Salon,
1 iron safe, bar outfit, in Violet
Springs & Fashion Salon in
Lexington, OT; Bill of Sale; Frank P.
Cease, probate judge.

1:271 Donohoe, W.H. & R.R. (his wife)

49

from Temple, Bell Co., Texas to
Armstrong, C.W.; Feb 18, 1891;
Jun 1892; Lot 13 & 14 Blk 65 in
Norman, OT by patent from U.S
government; Warranty Deed.

1:272　Pollock, Josie & David (her husband)
to Craig, C.A.; Apr 22, 1892; Jun 9,
1892; Lot 7 Blk 6 in Norman, OT;
Warranty Deed.

1:273　Rhymes, P.A. & Vicenda (his wife)
to Eslick, J.W.; Nov 3, 1890; Jun 11,
1892; Lot 17 Blk 35 in Norman, OT;
Warranty Deed; Lizzie Eslick.

1:274　Jasper, James R. to Trustees of Twp
8 North Range 1 West; Vandver, J.;
Hall, Abe; Slayter, J.H.; Hodam, F.T.
& Gatewood, G.B.F.; Aug 31, 1891;
Jun 11,1892; 1 acre NW4 corner of
NW4　Sec 25 T8N R1W for the
benefit of School District; Quit Claim
Deed; Newman, A.J. & T.E.
Wilkins.

1:275　Hughs, William H. to Trustees of
Twp 8N Range 1W; Vandver,

50

J.; Hall, Abe; Slayter, J.H.; Hodam,
F.T. & Gatewood, G.B.F.; Aug 22,
1891; Jun 11, 1892; 1 acre NE2 of
Sec 26 T8N R1W for the benefit of
school district;Quit Claim Deed;
F.T. Hodam & W.W. Hays.

1:276 Hoffmann, August to Trustees of
Twp 8N Range 1 W; Vandver, J.;
Hall, Abe; Slayter, J.H.; Hodam, F.T.
& Gatewood, G.B.F.; Aug 22, 1891;
Jun 11, 1892; 2 acres in square form
SE corner of SE2 Sec 5 T8N R1W
for the benefit of School District;
Quit Claim Deed; L.L. McComb &
T.M. Ritchesom.

1:277 Carver, John F. to Trustees of Twp
8N Range 1W; Vandver, J.; Hall,
Abe; Slayter, J.H.; Hodam, F.T.
& Gatewood, G.B.F.; Aug 22, 1891;
Jun 11, 1892; 4 acres in square form
NE4 of Sec 7 T8N R1W for the
benefit of School District; Quit
Claim Deed; W.W. Hays & R.A.
McClellan.

1:278 Appleby, William H. to Trustees of

51

Twp 8N Range 1W; Vandver, J.;
Hall, Abe; Slayter, J.H.; Hodam, F.T.
& Gatewood, G.B.F; Aug 21, 1891;
Jun 11, 1892; 2 acres in SE4 of Sec
20 T8N R1W for the benefit of
School District; Quit Claim Deed;
Viola & Carrie Appleby.

1:279 Colley, George H. & Josie M. (his
wife) to Thomas, David M.; Jun 15,
1892; Jun 15, 1892; Part of NW
corner of NW2 Sec 29 T9N part of
Colley homestead; (no range stated);
Warranty Deed.

1:280 Snook, Charles S. to T.M.
Richardson Lumber Company of
Oklahoma Co., OT; Jun 14, 1892;
Jun 14, 1892; Lots 18 to 20 Blk 49
in Norman, OT; Warranty Deed;
B.N. Woodson.

1:281 Clare, J.D. & Mary E. (his wife) to
Terry, T.M.; Apr 13, 1892; Lot 3 &
4 Blk 48 in Norman, OT; Warranty
Deed.

1:282 McKee, Robert B. & Ida V. (his

wife) of "B" County, Oklahoma
Territory to Asher, William R.;
Jun 23, 1892; Jun 24, 1892; Lots 30-
32 Blk 16 in Norman, OT; Not
part of McKee homestead; Warranty
Deed.

1:283   Owens, S.B. & Etta (his wife) to
        Stuart, John M. & Walker, Durward;
        Jul 2, 1892; Jul 2, 1892; SW one acre
        of Owen Addition Blk "W";
        Warranty Deed.

1:284   Williams, William S. to Williams,
        John P.; Jun 25, 1892; Jun 25, 1892;
        Lots 8 & 9 of Blk 72 in Norman,
        OT; Warranty Deed.

1:285   Cease, Frank P. & Minnie C. (his
        wife) to Capshaw, M.T.J.; Jul 12,
        1892; Jul 12, 1892; Lots 7 & 8 Blk
        3 in Colleys 2nd Addition in
        Norman, OT; Warranty Deed.

1:286   Barker, Winfield C. & Margaret E.
        (his wife) to Boyle, Eugene; Jul 11,
        1892; Jul 11, 1892; SE4 Sec 6 T3W
        R10N; 160 acres, homestead of

Barker; Warranty Deed; Edgar N.
Sweet & J.R. Harvey.

1:287 Woods, R.W. to Flood, John H.; Nov
18, 1890; Lots 15 & 16 in Blk 71 of
Norman, OT; Warranty Deed.

1:288 Lane, James W. & A.E. (his wife) to
Shroyer, Frank B.; Jul 23, 1892; Jul
25, 1892; NE4 Sec 10 T10N R2W
160 acres; sellers can not write;
Warranty Deed.

1:289 McGinley, Michael adm of estate of
James Fitzgerald, dec'd to Borah,
Mrs. J.E.; Jul 25, 1892; Jul 25, 1892;
Lots 11 & 12 & 19-22 in Blk 84
in Norman, OT; Adm Deed; E.E.
Hennessy.

1:290 Murray, E.W. of Purcell, IT to
Murray, J.A. (wife of E.W. Murray)
of Purcell, IT; Aug 6, 1892; Aug 6,
1892; Lots 5 & 6 in Blk 56 in
Lexington, OT; Warranty Deed.

1:291 Driver, Mrs. Adaline of Rockwell
Co., Texas to Gotcher, James P.; Jun

6, 1892; SE4 of Sec 30 & Sec 29
T9N R2W; Warranty Deed.

1:292 Allen, Clem W. & Almira V. (his
wife) of Canadian Co., OT to
Howarth, M.L. & Hallmark, W.A.;
Aug 12, 1892; Lot 4 in Blk 45 in
Norman, OT; Warranty Deed;
C.E. Hunter.

1:293 Storrier, D.L. & Helen (his wife) to
McCarty, Jerry; Aug 4, 1892; Lot 17
& 18 in Blk 33 in Norman, OT;
Helen Storrier in Omandaga Co, NY
on Aug 1, 1892; Warranty Deed.

1:294 Grimmett, H. & M. (his wife) from
Atoka Co., IT to Harrington, C.A.;
Aug 10, 1892; Lots 1- 4 in Blk 15
in T.R. Waggoner's 1st Addition to
Norman, OT; Warranty Deed;
James P. Addison & S.P. Aucker.

1:295 Garvin, S.J. & Susan (his wife) to
McLane, H.H. of Pickens County,
Chickasaw Nation, IT; Apr 1892;
Jun 1, 1892; Lots 7, 12 & 22 in Blk
16 in Noble, OT; Warranty Deed.

1:296   Marr, N. & S.M. (his wife) to
        Randolph, Daniel & Alice; Aug 25,
        1892; Aug 25, 1892; NE4 Sec 21
        T8N R2W; Release of Mortgage.

1:297   Randolph, Daniel & Alice (his wife)
        to Martin, Mary C.; Aug 25, 1892;
        Aug 25, 1892; NE4 Sec 21 T8N
        R2W; Warranty Deed.

1:298   Andrews, Mary E. to Haws, A.D.;
        Aug 26, 1892; NW4 SE4 Sec 6 T6N
        R1W; Andrews from Union City, OT
        & Haws from Purcell, IT; Indenture;
        release filed Bk. 3, pg 241.

1:300   Harding, Charles A. & Mary M. (his
        wife) to Hodges, John; Aug 20,
        1892; Lots 17 & 18, Blk 3, Larsh 1st
        Addition in Norman, OT; Hardings
        from Butler Co., Kansas; Warranty
        Deed.

1:301   Gilleck, W.T. & Mary B. (his wife)
        to Lefors, Rufus; Aug 20, 1892; Lots
        8-15, Blk 5, Bowling 1st Addition in
        Norman, OT; Warranty Deed.

1:302 Elkins, Mattie B. & Charles (her
husband) to Williams, S.L.; July 30,
1892; Lot 20, Blk 42, Lexington,
OT; Indenture; release signed when
paid Sept.. 6, 1892.

1:303 Bondurant, J.D. & Myrah Gray (his
wife) to Miller, J.M.; Feb 10, 1892;
Lots 4-16, Blk 44, Lexington, OT;
All parties in Louisville, Jefferson
Co., KY; Warranty Deed; see Bk. 1,
pg. 423 - excepting lots 1 to 3.

1:305 Porter, J.H. (a single man) to
Minnear, William T.; Aug 24, 1892;
Lot 2, Blk 26 & Lot 9, Blk 33 in
Norman, OT; Porter of Platt Co.,
Missouri; Warranty Deed.

1:307 Bonstead, R.H. & Julia F. (his wife)
to Forehand, Hugh L.; June 18,1892;
Lots 1-2, Blk 56, Lexington, OT;
Bonsteads from Chickasaw Nation,
IT; Warranty Deed; John W.
Medearis & H.W. Stuart.

1:308 Burns, G.W. & Edith (his wife) to
Ewart, R.J.; Sept 1, 1892; Lot 1-2,

57

Blk 43, Norman, OT; Warranty
Deed.

1:309   Owens, S.B. & Etta (his wife) to
        Bellamy, William H.; Aug 31, 1892;
        1 acre in NW corner NE4 Sec 29
        T9N   R2W; Warranty Deed.

1:310   Sconce, J. M. & Cassender (his wife)
        to Owens, S.B. & Etta (his wife);
        Aug 31, 1892; part of NE4 Sec 29
        T9N   R2W;   Warranty Deed.

1:311   Hocker, W.E. to Elkins, Mattie B.;
        July 18, 1892; Lot 20, Blk 42
        Lexington , OT; Hocker of Sacred
        Heart, OT; Warranty Deed.

1:312   Cannon, J.S. & Hattie (his wife) to
        Wood, V.A.; Sept 9, 1892; Lots 27
        & 28 Blk 9 Waggoner's 1st
        Addition to Norman, OT; Cannons
        are from McDonough Co., Illinois;
        Warranty Deed.

1:313   Smith, George "the Sheriff" to
        Tester, B.F.; Aug 29, 1892; Lot 5 to
        10 Blk 34 in Norman, OT; J.M.

Ragsdale, Ed Corett, & C.R.
McClain debtors; Sheriff's Deed.

1:314 Saxon, J.W. & Mattie J. (his wife)
from "B" County, O.T. to Saxon,
M.W. & wife; May 30, 1892; Lots
17 & 18 Blk 61 in Noble, OT;
Warranty Deed; Will H. Clark &
N.F. Hewett.

1:315 Isom, W.M. to White, J.E.; Sept 30,
1892; Lots 4 to 16 in Blk 69 & Lot
16 in Blk 54 of Lexington, OT;
Quit Claim Deed; H.T. Snow.

1:316 Dollmeier, Mike & Josefine (his wife)
& Billen, Peter & Barbary (his wife)
of Barton Co., Kansas to Penny,
Everett C.; Sept 15, 1892; Lots 3 &
4 & S2 of NW4 Sec 5 T10N R3W;
Warranty Deed.

1:317 Oden, S.J. & F.O. (his wife) from
Palo Pinto Co., Texas to Gray, J.F.;
Oct 4, 1892; Lots 1-16 in Blk 18 in
T.R. Waggoner's First Addition to
Norman, OT; Warranty Deed.

1:318 T.M. Richardson Lumber Company
& T.M. Richardson & D.C.
Richardson (his wife) to Little, J.S.;
Jun 29, 1892; Lots 25 Blk 42 in
Lexington, OT; Warranty Deed.

1:319 Beale, Andrew J. & Mary A. (his
wife) from Oklahoma Co., OT to
Applegate, Henry; Oct 13, 1892;
NW4 Sec15 T10N R3W;
Warranty Deed.

1:320 Brown, Jim & Zora (his wife) to
Thomas, Mary L.; Oct 12, 1892;
E2 S2 SW4 of SW4 Sec 20 T9N
R2W, 10 acres; Warranty Deed.

1:321 Thomas, J.W. & Anna (his wife) to
Thomas, D.M.; Oct 12, 1892;W2 S2
SE4 SW4 Sec 20 T9N R2W; 10
acres; Warranty Deed.

1:322 Renfrow, W.C. & Jennie B. (his wife)
to Thomas, David M.; Oct 15, 1892;
Lots 15 & 16 in Blk 23 in Norman,
OT; Warranty Deed.

1:323 Renfrow, W.C. & Jennie B. (his wife

to Thomas, David M.; Oct 15, 1892;
SW4 SW4 SW4 Sec 20 T9N R2W;
10 acres; Warranty Deed.

1:324 Colley, George H. & Josie M. (his
wife) to Womack, D.B.; Oct
24, 1892; Part of Lot 14 Blk 1 in
Colly's 2nd Addition of Norman, OT;
Warranty Deed.

1:325 Colley, George H. & Josie M. (his
wife) to Thomas, Mrs. Anna; Oct 24,
1892; part of Blk 1 Colley's 2nd
Addition to Norman, OT; Warranty
Deed.

1:326 Lefors, Rufus & Fannie (his wife) to
Choate, W.L.; Oct 20, 1892; Lots 8-
15 in Blk 5 in Bowling's 1st Addition
to Norman, OT; Warranty Deed.

1:327 Renfrow, W.C. & Jennie B. (his wife)
to Eslick, John I.; Oct 1892; Lots
17-20 in Blk 14 in Norman, OT;
Warranty Deed.

1:328 Condon, Thomas D. (single) to
Renfrow, W.C.; Oct 10, 1892;

NE4 Sec19 T9N R2W; Warranty
Deed; F. Caruthers.

1:329 Thomas, D.M., Sr. and Mary S.
(his wife) to Brown, Mrs. Lora;
Oct 12, 1892; 1/2 interest in Lot 11
Blk 6 in Norman, OT; maybe Zora
Brown; Warranty Deed.

1:330 Lefors, Rufus & Fannie (his wife) to
Thomas, J.W.; Oct 17, 1892; Part of
NW4 Sec 29 T9N R2W; Warranty
Deed.

1:331 Smith, Lucy & Neil (her husband) to
Prigmore, D.H.; Aug 11, 1892;
Lot 8 Blk 65 in Lexington, OT;
Warranty Deed; H.W. Stuart & D.B.
Easton.

1:332 Cox, James A. (single) to Hewitt,
Lee D. of Christain Co., Illinois;
Oct 29, 1892; NE4 Sec 17 T10N
R4W; Warranty Deed; Hugh H.
Hillman.

1:333 Cox, James D. & Mary C. (his wife)
to Hewitt, Lee D. of Christian Co.,

Illinois; Oct 29, 1892; SE4 Sec 17
T10N R4W; Warranty Deed;
Hugh H. Hillman.

1:334 Richardson, W.C.W. agent for T.M.
Richardson Lumber Company to
Blackiston, T.J.; Nov 4, 1892;
Part of SW corner of SW4 Sec 21
T9N R2W; 1 acre; Warranty Deed.

1:335 Johnson, T.J. & M.F. (his wife) to
Arnold, D.S. from Antioch,
Missouri; Nov 25, 1892; Part of
SW4 Sec 21 T9N R2W; 41
acres more or less; Warranty Deed.

1:336 Waits, Dr. S.A. & Stella J. (his wife)
to Corn, J.M. & Hanah (his wife);
Nov 21, 1892; Part of Lots A, B, C
Blk 70 also Lots 1-4 in Blk 70 in
D.L. Larsh's 1st Addition in Norman,
OT; Warranty Deed.

1:337 Thomas, D.M., Sr. & Mary L. (his
wife) to Thomas, D.M. Jr.; Nov 12,
1892; Part of NW4 Sec 29 T9N
R2W; 1 acre tract; Warranty Deed.

1:338   Sanders, C.R. & M.C. (his wife) of
        Clay Co., Texas to Lefors, Rufus;
        Nov 4, 1892; Lots 9 & 10 in Blk 4 in
        Colley's 2nd Addition of Norman,
        OT; Warranty Deed.

1:339   Carder, Frederick & Nancy E. (his
        wife) to Roberts, J.J.; Nov 4, 1892;
        SE4 Sec8 T8N R2W; Warranty
        Deed.

1:340   Frazey, Emily F. & George W. (her
        husband) to Marr, N.; Nov 7, 1892;
        N2 of NW4 Sec 27 T9N R1W;
        Warranty Deed.

1:341   Lindermann, Henry (single man) to
        Little, Woodward; Oct 26, 1892;
        E2 of NW4 Sec 10 T6N R1W;
        Warranty Deed; W.S. Field.

1:342   Lefors, Rufus & Fannie (his wife) &
        D.M & Mary L. Thomas (his wife)
        to Cathey, J.W.; Nov 12,1892;
        Lots 1 & 2 Blk 52 in Norman, OT;
        Warranty Deed.

1:343   Marr, N. & Lillian (his wife) to

Mahaney, George S.; Nov 9, 1892;
Lots 7 & 8 Blk 3 Colley's 1st
Addition of Norman, OT; Warranty
Deed.

1:344   Bondurant, J.D. & Myrah Gray
Bondurant (his wife) of Jefferson
Co., Kentucky to Beishouse, Frank;
Oct 17, 1892; Lots 3 & 4 Blk 59 &
Lots 5 & 6 in Blk 60; Myrah Gray
Bondurant New York Co., New
York; Warranty Deed.

1:345   Lefors, Rufus & Fannie (his wife) to
Lewis, A.J.; Dec 1, 1892; Lots 9 &
10 in Blk 4 Colley's 2nd Addition
of Norman, OT; Warranty Deed.

1:346   Williams, B.T. & E.H. (his wife) to
Johnson, T.J. & M.F. (his wife);
Sep 23, 1892; Lot 2 Blk 1 in his
claim dated June 26, 1892; Quit
Claim Deed.

1:347   Christy, James A. & Margaret (his
wife) to Bingham, Elenora &
children; Nov 11, 1892; NW4 Sec 14
T6N   R1W; Cristys from Carrol

Co., Missouri; "for love &
affection"; Warranty Deed; Sam B.
Robertson.

1:348 Essex, Frank W. to Trustees for Dist.
       #4 School, H. Downing, A.O.
       McGill, W.E. Clanton, J.L. Adair;
       Oct 18, 1892; 1 acre in NE4 Sec 26
       T9N R3W; For benefit of school;
       Quit Claim Deed.

1:349 Hasness, James (single man) to
       Mohr, Nicolas; Dec 7, 1892; Dec 9,
       1892; Lot 1 & 2 & S2 NE4 Sec 2
       T10N R4W; "Correction deed
       dated April 3, 1897"; Warranty
       Deed.

1:350 Smith, Elizabeth (widow) to Newell,
       T.J.; Nov 22, 1892; Lots 1, Blk 1,
       Colleys 1st Addition to Norman,
       OT; Mrs. Smith of Oklahoma Co.,
       OT; Warranty Deed.

1:351 Jones, J.A. & Sallie (his wife) to
       Jones, Hughbert; Dec 7, 1892;
       Numerous lots totaling 57.77 acres
       in part of Sec 30 T9N R2W;

Original deed recorded Bk 1, pg 264; Warranty Deed; T. Caruthers.

1:353 Johnson, T.J. & M.F. (his wife) to Cathey, W.W.; Dec 3, 1892; Portion of SW4 Sec 21 T9N R2W; Lots 2-4, Blk 1, Johnson's Claim; Warranty Deed.

1:354 Elledge, W.N. & Nora (his wife) to Hart, W.H. & Elland, E.; Dec 14, 1892; Lots 15, Blk 13, Norman, OT; Warranty Deed.

1:355 Peltier, Robert F. & Victoria (his wife) to Bowers, Athy T.; Dec 7, 1892; NW4 Sec 8 T6N R1E; Bowers from Cleburne Co., Texas; Land represents original patent for Peltier who is "member or citizen of Pottawattomie Tribe"; Warranty Deed.

1:356 McGee, J.D. to Jackson, J.M.; Mar 24, 1892; Lot 15-16, Blk 65, Norman, OT; McGee is in Waldo, Columbia Co., Arkansas; Warranty Deed.

1:357   Mitchell, A.J. & Elizabeth (his wife)
        to Wynne, D.H.; Dec 14, 1892;
        Lots 19-20, Blk 12, Norman, OT;
        Warranty Deed.

1:358   Teeter, Benjamin F. & Nancy L. (his
        wife) to Anderson, Matthew L.;
        Dec 24, 1892; Lots 9-10, Blk 34,
        Norman, OT; Warranty Deed.

1:359   Briggs, Levi L. & Narcissus (his
        wife) to Briggs, W.W.; Dec 17,
        1892; Jan 3, 1893; Lots 3-5, Blk 73,
        and Lots 5-6, Blk 51 in Norman,
        OT; Warranty Deed; J.M. Hall &
        T.W. Briggs.

1:360   Runyan, R.M. & Lelia (his wife) to
        Woodard, C.P.; Dec 26, 1892;
        Lots 4-6, Blk 47, Norman, OT;
        Warranty Deed.

1:361   Colley, George H. & Josie M. (his
        wife) to King, M.A.; Jan 2, 1893;
        Part of NW4 Sec 29 T9N R2W;
        Warranty Deed.

1:362   Jones, J.A & Sallie (his wife) to

Caruthers, F.; Nov 22, 1892;
Lots 12-16 Blk 1 in Norman, OT;
Warranty Deed.

1:363 Colley, Josie M. & George H. (her
husband) to Worley, A.J.; Feb 20,
1893; Lots 1-3 Blk 47 in Norman,
OT; Warranty Deed.

1:364 Colley, George H. & Josie M. (his
wife) to Worley, A.J.; Feb 20, 1893;
part of Lot 1 Blk 3 Colley's 2nd
Addition to Norman, OT; Warranty
Deed.

1:365 Colley, George H. & Josie M. (his
wife) to Worley, A.J.; Feb 20, 1893;
Lots 7 - 10 & 15 & 16 Blk 5 & Lots
11-15 in Colley's 2nd Addition of
Norman, OT; Warranty Deed.

1:366 Colley, George H. & Josie M. (his
wife) to Worley, A.J.; Feb 20, 1893;
Part of lot 14 Blk 1 Colley's 1st
Addition of Norman, OT; Warranty
Deed.

1:367 Berry, Georgia A. & Thomas E. (her

husband) to Vincent, Mary C.;
Feb 8, 1893; Lots 1-4 Blk 30 in
Norman, OT; Warranty Deed.

1:368   Davis, J.H. (single man) to T.M.
Richardson Lumber Co.; Feb 28,
1893; Lot 27 Blk 46 in Lexington,
OT; Warranty Deed; H.H. Bradbury
& G.C. Grimstead.

1:369   Zimmerson, George W. & Jerlean to
Bowman, Julian; Dec 24, 1892;
All of Blk 61 in Norman, OT;
Warranty Deed.

1:370   Vincent, Thomas (single man) to
Warner, George (from Sanders Co,
Nebraska); Jan 17, 1893; SW4 Sec 5
T8N R2W;160 acres; Warranty
Deed.

1:371   Brisco, Alfred (single man) to Harris,
S.H.; Mar 22, 1893; Lot 5 Blk 65 in
Norman, OT; Warranty Deed.

1:372   Patton, John G. & Annie M. (his
wife) to Minor, D.A.; Feb 20, 1893;
Lots 11 & 12 Blk 3 in Norman, OT;

Lien on title; Statuary Deed.

1:373 Webb, Mrs. N.E. (femme sole),
       Bowen, Violet & John W. (her
       husband) from Dallas Co., Texas to
       Wilson, Jesse A. from Davis Co.,
       Missouri; Feb 10, 1893; Lots 5 & 6
       Blk 53 in Norman, OT; Warranty
       Deed.

1:375 White, James E. to Isom, W.M.;
       Dec 1, 1892; Lots 4 -16 in Blk 69 &
       Lot 16 Blk 54 in Lexington, OT;
       Quit Claim Deed; H.T. Snow.

1:376 Colley, George H. & Josie M. (his
       wife) to Sullivant, Jesse; Sep 2,
       1892; Part of NE corner lot 15 Blk 1
       Colley's 1st Addition to Norman, OT;
       Warranty Deed.

1:378 Keller, E.J. to Fawcett, N.E.; Jul 9,
       1891; Lot 1-8 Blk 81 in Lexington,
       OT; Paid with two horses no cash;
       Warranty Deed; J.W. Marcum &
       E.M. Abernathy.

1:379 Draper, Bessie I. & Charles M. (her

husband) to Teel, Charles F.; Feb 21,
1893; Lots 9 & 10 in Blk 1 in
Norman. OT; Warranty Deed.

1:380   Thomas, D.M., Sr. & Mary L. (his
        wife) to Thomas, D.M., Jr. from
        Tarrant Co., Texas; Jan 6, 1893;
        1/2 acre of land part of NW4 Sec 29
        T9N   R2W; Warranty Deed.

1:381   Owens, S.B. & Etta (his wife) to
        Chapman, W.L. & Jones, J.A.;
        Jan 18, 1893; 1 acre of land Blk A
        in Owens Addition part of Sec 29
        T9N   R2W; Warranty Deed.

1:382   Jones, Hughbert & Mary E. (his
        wife) to Anderson, Matthew L.;
        Jan 7, 1893; Lots 5 & 6 Blk 1 of J.A.
        Jones 1st Addition of Norman, OT;
        Warranty Deed.

1:383   Jones, James A. & Sallie (his wife) to
        Anderson, Matthew L.; Mar 2, 1893;
        Lots 5-12 Blk 7 J.A. Jones 1st
        Addition of Norman, OT; Warranty
        Deed.

1:384 Brisco, John & Adaline (his wife)
from Hancock Co, Iowa to S.W.
Gorden & B.F. Gorden; Jan 26,
1893; Lots 31, 32 & 33 in Blk 7 of
Norman, OT; Warranty Deed.

1:385 Archambault, Fred & Josephine (his
wife) to Avey, Harry; Oct 25, 1892;
Lots 25 - 32 in Blk 10 in Lexington,
OT; Warranty Deed; Neil Smith.

1:386 Collins, J.M. & Phoebe (his wife)
from Grayson Co., Texas to
Chapman, L.C. from Grayson Co.,
Texas; Jul 16, 1892; Lots 1 & 4 in
Blk 65 in Norman, OT; Warranty
Deed with vendor lien.

1:387 DeWitt, W.H. & Roberter (his wife)
to Denham, Dreny & Denison,
Henry; Jan 25, 1893; Part of NE
corner Sec31 T9N R2W; 1 acre;
Warranty Deed.

1:389 Campbell, C.W. & Elizabeth (his
wife) of Purcell, IT, carpenter &
McKilvey, J.S. & Abbie E. from
Moscow Mills, Ohio, farmer to

Bowles, John; Dec 6, 1892; Lots 10
Blk 84 in Norman, OT; Indenture;
Grant Green & Feorgicer Newton.

1:391 Keller, E.J. from Lexington, OT to
Cramon, Lewis from Lexington, OT;
Nov 3, 1891; Lots 17, 18 & 21-24 in
Blk 25 of Lexington, OT; Warranty
Deed.

1:392 Wolf, George F. & Anna L. (his
wife) to Bessent, C.H., agent; Jan
20, 1893; Lots 3 & 4 in Blk 40 in
Noble, OT;   Warranty Deed.

1:393 Flood, E.O. & Emma (his wife) to
Carder, Frederick; Mar 8, 1893;
Lot 28 & 29 Blk 73 of Norman,O.T.;
Warranty Deed.

1:394 Worley, A.J. & Lori S. (his wife) to
Patterson, L.M.; Mar 6, 1893; Lots
15 & 16 in Blk 5 Colley 2nd
Addition of Norman, OT; Warranty
Deed.

1:395 Bowling, C.G. & Alice (his wife) to
Gribble, Mrs. M.F.; Aug 5, 1892;

Lots 3 - 7 in Blk 8 in Bowlings 1ˢᵗ Addition of Norman, OT; Warranty Deed.

1:396   Booker, Philip W. to T.M. Richardson Lumber Company; Feb 20, 1893; Lots 23- 26 Blk 46 in Lexington, O.T.; Warranty Deed; Llewelyn Gwynne.

1:397   Hamilton, J.C. & May (his wife) to Rory, Vallie E., Groy, Robert F. & Verian, James R.; Dec 20, 1892; Lot 30 in Blk 42 in Lexington, O.T.; Warranty Deed; Nettie Mosley & H.W. Stewart.

1:398   Keller, E.J. & Jessie (his wife) to Booker, Philip W.; Feb 20, 1893; Lots 23-26 in Blk 46 in Lexington, O.T.; Warranty Deed; J.S. Bryant.

1:399   Williamson, Thomas M. & L.M. (his wife) to Vanderford, John A.; Mar 2, 1893; SW4 Sec 4 T10N R4W; 160 acres more or less; Warranty Deed.

1:400   Carnahan, S.P. (single man) to

VanBuskirk, Carrie E. from Cowley
Co., Kansas; Aug 11, 1891; S2 of
NW 4 Sec 7 T6N R1W; Notary in
Butler Co., Kansas; Warranty Deed.

1:401 Mathis, T.B. & E.M. (his wife) to
McCarthy, D.C.; Mar 21, 1893;
SW4 Sec30 T9N R2W; Warranty
Deed.

1:402 Carlock, Jane (single) to Berry,
Thomas E.; Mar 17, 1893; Lot 14
Blk 7 in Norman, OT; Warranty
Deed; W.H. Airheart, W. Booth,
Edward Miller.

1:403 Marr, N. & L.M. (his wife) of
Colorado Springs, Colorado to
Frazy, George; Mar 11, 1893; N2 of
NW4 Sec 27 T9N R1W;
Quit Claim Deed.

1:404 Frazey, George W. & Emily T. (his
wife) to Gibbs, G.W.; Mar 7, 1893;
N2 of NW4 of Sec27 T9N R1W;
Warranty Deed.

1:405 Colley, George H. & Josie M. (his

wife) of Oklahoma County, OT to
Andrew, Robert & Allen, James;
Mar 21, 1893; Lot 1 & 2 & S2 of
NE4 Sec 1 T9N R3W; Randolph
Co., Illinois; Warranty Deed.

1:406 Robinson, Nathaniel & Elizabeth (his
wife) to Leach, Robert E.; Mar 27,
1893; N2 & N2 of S2 of SW4 Sec20
T9N R2W; 120 acres; Warranty
Deed; W.B. Lilsey & E.E.
Hennessy.

1:407 Exleton, Amelia & E.T. (her
husband) to Cranson, Lewis; Mar 10,
1893; Lots 29, 30 in Blk 47 in
Lexington, OT; Warranty Deed;
J.H. Davis & Neil Smith.

1:408 Cranson, Margaret H. to Cranson,
Lewis; Mar 24, 1893; Lots 19 & 20
in Blk 25 in Lexington, OT;
Warranty Deed; Neil Smith & A.
Cranson.

1:409 Weir, C.M. & Martha A. (his wife) to
Cranson, M.H.; Dec 26, 1891; Lots
19 & 20 in Blk 25 in Lexington, OT;

M.H. Cranson is female; Warranty
Deed; J.B. Morrison.

1:410   Bowling, C.G. & Alice (his wife) to
        McGinley, M.; Mar 16, 1893; Lots 5
        & 6 in Blk 3 of C.G. Bowling 1st
        Addition of Norman, OT; Warranty
        Deed.

1:411   Banks, David F. & Sarah E. (his
        wife) to Craig, Martha J.; Mar 28,
        1893; Lot 13 in Blk 23 of Norman,
        OT; Warranty Deed; Medd L. Miser
        & John S. Allan.

1:412   Brown, Alice & James (her husband)
        to Jeffers, Raymond; Aug 6, 1892;
        Lot 30 in Blk 38 in Lexington, OT;
        Warranty Deed.

1:413   Ingram, J.H. & Elvira (his wife) to
        Nesbitt, J.W.; Sep 3, 1892; Lot 31 &
        32 in Blk 27 in Lexington, OT;
        Signed by mark Elvira; Warranty
        Deed; A. Hutchin.

1:414   Faris, Sallie T. & Joseph A. (her
        husband) to Hall, Survilla E. from

Grayson Co., Texas; Oct 13,
1892; Lot 30 & 31 in Blk 65 in
Norman, OT; Sallie T. Faris was
Sallie T. Herronymus before
marriage from Pontotoc Co.,
Chickasaw Nation, IT; Warranty
Deed; William A. Monroe & Bettie
Monroe.

1:415   Worley, Andrew J. & Lou S. (his
        wife) to Bowden, B.A. & Martin,
        Minnie C; Apr 1, 1893; Lots 9 & 10
        in Blk 5 & Lot 14 in Blk 2 all in
        Colley's 2nd Addition of Norman,
        OT; Warranty Deed; John S. Allan.

1:417   Brooks, Homer & Mary L. (his wife)
        to Carder, Frederick; Mar 27, 1893;
        S1/6 of Lots 17 to 19 Blk 5 in
        Norman, OT; Mary Brooks in Adair
        County, Iowa; Warranty Deed.

1:419   Johnson, T.J. & M.F. (his wife) to
        Lane, J.P.; Apr 12, 1893; 47.58 acres
        of SW4 Sec 21 T9N R2W;
        Warranty Deed.

1:420   Green, C.M. to Dwytel, Patrick from

Mason, Co., Kentucky; Apr 16, 1892; Lots 13-16 in Blk 16 in Lexington, OT; bought from townsite board #4 trustees; Warranty Deed; C.H. Barlow.

1:421 Averyt, A.N. & Maddie C. (his wife) to Bishop, T.M.; Apr 3, 1893; Lots 19, 20 in Blk 31 in Norman, OT; Warranty Deed.

1:422 Vivian, George R. to Davidson, Lula S.; Mar 6, 1893; Lots 22, 23, 25, 26 in Blk 27 in Lexington, OT; Warranty Deed; Llew Gwynne.

1:423 Davis, J.H. to Weitzenhoffer & Turk; Apr 18, 1893; Lots 29 & 30 in Blk 41 in Lexington, OT; Warranty Deed.

1:424 Synnott, Ellen & Edward (her husband) to Phillips, George L.; Apr 21, 1893; SW4 Sec28 T9N R2W; 4 acres of land; Warranty Deed.

1:425 Sylva, Nate & Hattie to Robinson,

Elizabeth; Apr 24, 1893; SE4 Sec 5
T7N R1W; Warranty Deed;
R.J. Edwards.

1:426 Mason, Lemuel L. & Virginia (his
wife) to Copaugh, Elizabeth; Apr 11,
1893; Lots 17, 18 21, 22 in Blk 5 of
Lexington, OT; Warranty Deed.

1:427 Taylor, E. & D. (husband & wife) to
Wolf, George F. & Anne L.; Mar 14,
1893; All Lots 27, 28, Blk 40 in
Noble, OT; Warranty Deed.

1:429 Cornell, Smith P. & Ella J. of Lincoln
Co., OT to Whitford, Romanzo B.;
Mar 25, 1893; Lot 1-32 Blk 12
in Noble, OT; Warranty Deed.

1:430 Bowling, C.G. & Alice (his wife) to
Methodist Episcopal Church South
Trustees, J.M. Chastain, J. P.
Jackson, J.E. Turner, W.H. Seawell,
J.A. Jones; May 4, 1893; 6 acres in
NE4 of Sec 29 T9N R2W; Land to
be used for M.E. Church South
School; Warranty Deed.

1:431 Kittredge, John H. to Kittredge,
       Emma; May 4, 1893; SW4 Sec 5
       T9N R3W; Warranty Deed.

1:432 Hall, J.H. (a single man) to Hall, John
       W.; Jan 30, 1893; Lots 6 & 7, Blk
       12, Norman, OT; Quit Claim Deed.

1:433 Owens, S.B. & Etta (his wife) to
       Steele, George H.; May 6, 1893;
       Part of NE4 Sec 29 T9N R2W aka
       N/2 Blk 6, Owens Addition,
       Norman, OT; Warranty Deed.

1:434 Colley, George H. & Josie M. (his
       wife) to Dunham, J.C.; May 9, 1893;
       Lot 1, Blk 5, Colley's 2nd Addition of
       Norman, OT; Warranty Deed;
       C.Q. Rood.

1:435 Mitchell, A.J. & Lizzie (his wife) to
       Thomas, D.M. & Carder, Frederick;
       May 11, 1893; Lots 15 & 16, Blk 22,
       Norman, OT; Warranty Deed.

1:436 Gauge, Amanda to Hughes, John H.;
       May 4, 1893; About 80 acres in E/2
       NW/4 Sec 35 T7N R1W; Amanda

may be Amduda; Warranty Deed.

1:437 Spitzer, J. & Ida J. (his wife) to
Watts, William A.; May 15, 1893;
Lots 21 & 22, Blk 33, Norman, OT;
Warranty Deed; Sam Turk & Sam
Goodman.

1:438 Wiseham, Gerhard W. to Allen, E.D.;
May 9, 1893; Lots 30-32, Blk 14,
and Lots 15, 16, 19 & 20, Blk 4, and
Lots 26-29, Blk 53, and Lot 1, Blk
2, and Lots 13-16, Blk 2, all in
Norman, OT; Warranty Deed.

1:439 Criswell, J.C. & Nancy (his wife) of
Cooke Co., Texas to Criswell, J.R.
of Cooke Co., Texas; Mar 13, 1893;
Lots 8 & 15, Blk 4, and Lot 16, Blk
3 Colley's 2nd Addition, Norman,
OT; Warranty Deed.

1:440 Garnand, D.L. & Mary (his wife) of
Garland Co., Arkansas to Garnand,
James F.; Mar 1, 1893; Lots 25-28,
Blk 2, Norman, OT; Warranty Deed.

1:441 Gray, John F. & Arena (his wife) to

Howry, John H.; May 18, 1893;
Lot 1, Blk 72, Norman, OT;
Warranty Deed; Ollie Hodges & J.
Belden.

1:442 Haas, Reuben P. to Campbell,
Archibald S.; May 23, 1893;
Lot 3, Blk 51, Lexington, OT;
Quit Claim Deed.

1:443 Smith, Neil to Campbell, Archibald
S.; May 23, 1893; Lots 1 & 2, Blk
51, Lexington, OT; Quit Claim
Deed.

1:444 Anderson, Mary E. to Blackburn,
Ida; Mar 9, 1893; NW/4 SE/4 Sec 6
T6N R1W; Mary Anderson signs
in Canadian Co., OT; Warranty
Deed.

1:445 Munn, Edward T. (a single man) to
Anderson, M.L.; May 26, 1893;
Lots 11 & 12, Blk SW Four, Colley's
1st Addition of Norman, OT;
Warranty Deed.

1:446 Kingkade, Lucy T. & Andrew (her

husband) to Ferguson, John H.; May
31, 1893; Lot 12, Blk 5, Norman,
OT;   Warranty Deed.

1:447   Allen, W.D. & Emily L. (his wife) to
Downing, Hiram; June 3, 1893; 160
acres in the NW/4 Sec 28 T?N R3W;
Warranty Deed.

1:448   Davis, W.T. to Haddix, Ellen A.;
May 29, 1893; Lot 3 & 4, Blk 3,
Norman, OT; W.T. Davis signs in
Denton Co., Texas; Warranty Deed.

1:449   Rallston, W.W. & Alla E. (his wife)
from Brown Co., Kansas, to King,
David; May 31, 1893; 80 acres in S/2
SE/4 Sec 9 T9N R3W; Alla E.
Rallston signs in Lick Co., Indiana;
Warranty Deed.

1:450   Green, Mrs. May & S.S. (her
husband) to Blake, Nicholas; May
20, 1893; Lot 7, Blk 65,
Lexington, OT; Warranty Deed.

1:451   Blake, Nicholas to Houghton, T.R.
of Cowley Co., Kansas; May 25,

1893; Lot 7, Blk 65, Lexington, OT;
Quit Claim Deed; W.T. King & P.R.
Smith.

1:452   Owens, S.B. & Etta (his wife) to
        Roberts, E.J.; Feb 6, 1893; S/2 Blk
        K, Owens Addition, Norman {part of
        NE/4 Sec29-9N-2W}; Warranty
        Deed.

1:453   Terry, John W. & Kattie (his wife) to
        Terry, G.H.; Mar 28, 1893; 2 1/2
        acres in SE/4 Sec 29 T9N R2W;
        Warranty Deed.

1:454   Gorden, S.W. & Addie (his wife) to
        Terry, John W.; Apr 8, 1893; 10
        acres in a part of SE/4 Sec 29 T9N
        R2W; Replaces deed executed on
        June 6, 1892; Warranty Deed.

1:455   Brooks, Homer & Mary L. (his wife)
        of Adair Co., Iowa to Brooks, Willis
        E .; June 5, 1893; Part of Lot 17, Blk
        5, Norman, OT; Warranty Deed.

1:456   Goins, W.M. & Ada (his wife) to
        T.M. Richardson Lumber Co.; May

28, 1893; Lot 15 & 16, Blk 19,
Moore, OT.

1:457 Carrico, M.W. & Mary E. (his wife)
from Tarrant Co., Texas to
Burns, George W.; Jun 6, 1893; Lots
23 & 24 Blk 34 in Norman, OT;
Warranty Deed.

1:458 Trustees for the township of
Norman, OT; James M. Bishop,
Delbert L. Larsh & Samuel T. Leavy
to Berry, Robert C.; Dec 10, 1892;
W2 of SW4 Sec 29 T9N & R2W
& SE4 of Sec. 30, T9N, R2W;
Indenture.

1:461 Berry, Robert C. & Nora I. (his wife)
to Elledge, William N.; Dec 29,
1892; Lots 13 in Blk 5 in Norman,
OT; Warranty Deed.

1:462 Rennie, Albert of Wewoka, in
Seminole Nation, IT to Rennie,
Alexander from Denison, Texas; Apr
15, 1892; Lots 1, 2, 5 ,6 in BLK 45
in Noble, OT; Warranty Deed;
A.D. Matthews.

1:463   Eaton, S.A.D. & Irene P. (his wife)
         from Pocahontas, Arkansas to
         Talkington, Ella D.; Jun 24, 1893;
         Lots 9 - 12 in Blk 11 J.A. Jones
         Addition of Norman, OT;
         Warranty Deed.

1:464   Jones, J.A. & Sallie (his wife) to
         Eaton, S.A.D. & Irene P. (his wife)
         Mar 16, 1893; Lots 9 -12 in Blk 11
         of J.A. Jones Addition of Norman,
         OT; Warranty Deed.

1:465   Wilson, George & Maggie (his wife)
         to Briggs, L.L.; Dec 22, 1892; Lots
         15, 16 in Blk 1 in Colley's 1st
         Addition of Norman, OT; Warranty
         Deed.

1:466   Corette, Ed & Mary A. (his wife)
         from Cook Co., Illinois to Corette,
         Margaret; Jun 27, 1893; Lots 16, in
         Blk 5 in Norman, OT; Warranty
         Deed.

1:467   McConkey, W.A.M. & Mary A. (his
         wife) to McConkey, Justin; Mar 16,
         1893; Lots 5 - 8 in Blk 52 in Noble,

OT; Warranty Deed; R.B. Whitford.

1:468 Innis, Robert E. & Etta M. (his wife)
to Bellamy, William H.; Jun 24,
1893; Lots 25- 28 in Blk 55 in
Norman, OT; Warranty Deed.

1:469 Davis, J.H. to Hardwick, H.M.; Mar
1, 1893; Lots 29 -32 in Blk 22 in
Lexington, OT; Warranty Deed;
Neil Smith & H.T. Brown.

1:470 Ferguson, William H. & Nannie E.
(his wife) to Ferguson, John H.;
Jul 3, 1893; Part of SE corner of
NE4 Sec 31 T9N R2W; 2 acres;
Warranty Deed.

1:471 Myers, Washington L. & Lydia L.
(his wife) to Cowan, James; Jul 15,
1893; Lots 1, 2 & S2 NW4 Sec 7
T8N R1W; 156.66 acres;
Warranty Deed.

1:472 Johnson, E.B. & W.H. (her husband)
to Partridge, Mary E.; Jul 13, 1893;
Lot 17 in Blk 42 in Lexington, OT;
Warranty Deed; James Elkins & J.C.

Cashen.

1:473   Elledge, J.B. & Tenie (his wife) to
        Myers, Lydia L.; Jul 17, 1893;
        Lots 17 - 20 in Blk 46 in Norman,
        OT;   Warranty Deed.

1:474   Trustees of the townsite of Noble,
        OT, James M. Bishop, Delbert L.
        Larsh & Samuel T. Leavy to
        Southern Kansas Railway Co.;
        Jun 24, 1893; E2 Sec 27   T8N
        R2W;   right of way;   S.M. Moore.

1:477   Cowan, James & Elizabeth F. (his
        wife) to Myers, Washington L.;
        Jul 15, 1893; Lot 21 in Blk 46 in
        Norman, OT & part of SE4 Sec 29
        T9N   R2W;   Warranty Deed.

1:479   Blakney, B.B. (single man) from
        Pottawatomie Co., OT to Mann,
        William A.; Jul 10, 1893; Lots 27-
        29 in Blk 29 of the amended plat of
        Norman, OT;   Warranty Deed.

Index of People

B

Banks, David F., 78
Banks, Sarah E., 78
Banks, Varian, 33
Barker, Margaret E.,
53
Barker, Winfield C.,
53
Barlow, C.H., 80
Beale, Andrew J., 23,
60
Beale, Mary A., 60
Beale, Robert W., 23
Beaublossom, Jacob,
14
Beeler, George R., 33
Beeler, Georgie, 33
Beishause, Frank, 14
Beishouse, Frank, 65
Belcher, Mack, 13
Belcher, W.H, 12
Belden, J., 84
Belden, Z., 20
Beldeu, Julia, 8
Bell, James, 21
Bellamy, George, 18
Bellamy, William H.,
19, 20, 22, 58, 89
Bellamy, Wm. H., 25,
26
Bender, Peter A., 2
Benshouse, Frank, 28
Benton, O.H., 45

Berry, Addie, 3
Berry, Andrew A., 3
Berry, Georgia A., 69
Berry, Nora I., 87
Berry, Robert C., 87
Berry, T.E., 30
Berry, Thomas E., 69,
76
Bessent, C.H., 15, 18,
20, 46, 74
Bessent, Jennie E., 20
Bible, Solen A., 48
Billen, Barbary, 59
Billen, Peter, 31, 59
Bingham, Elenora, 65
Bish, James M., 38, 39
Bishop, J.B., 29
Bishop, James M., 87,
90
Bishop, T.M., 80
Bitsche, Edward, 23
Bitsche, Emily, 23
Black, Richard, 49
Blackburn, Ida, 84
Blackburn, W.C., 8
Blackburn, W.P., 40
Blackiston, T.J., 63
Blake, Ella, 29
Blake, George, 29
Blake, Mary E., 5, 29
Blake, Nicholas, 85
Blake, Tyler, 5, 29
Blakeney, B.B., 6, 40,
41

Blakney, B.B., 90
Boggs, B.L., 18
Boling, Alice, 43
Boling, C.G., 43
Bondurant, J.D., 12,
    14, 28, 57, 65
Bondurant, Myrah
    Gray, 14, 28, 57,
    65
Bonneau, Elizabeth,
    32
Bonneau, Salyone, 32
Bonstead, Julia F., 57
Bonstead, R.D., 18
Bonstead, R.H., 57
Booker, Philip W., 75
Booth, W., 76
Borah, Mrs. J.E., 54
Boston, James, 24
Bowden, B.A., 79
Bowen, John W., 71
Bowen, Violet, 71
Bowers, Athy T., 67
Bowie, H.T., 44
Bowles, John, 74
Bowling, Alice, 8, 10,
    35, 74, 78, 81
Bowling, C.G., 8, 10,
    35, 74, 78, 81
Bowman, Julian, 70
Boyle, Eugene, 53
Boyle, J.P., 27
Bradbury, H.H., 70
Brady, Frank, 15

Branhan, John, Estate
    of, 3
Briggs, L.L., 22, 24,
    88
Briggs, Levi L., 68
Briggs, Narcissus, 68
Briggs, T.W., 68
Briggs, W.W., 68
Brisco, Adaline, 73
Brisco, Alfred, 70
Brisco, John, 73
Briscoe, J.S., 6
Brittain, M.L., 3
Brock, Allie, 29
Brooks, Homer, 79, 86
Brooks, Mary L., 79,
    86
Brooks, Willis E., 86
Brown, Alice, 78
Brown, H.T., 89
Brown, Helen L., 41
Brown, James, 78
Brown, Jim, 60
Brown, Lina, 35, 36
Brown, Mrs. Lora, 62
Brown, Mrs. Zora, 62
Brown, Samuel H., 35,
    36
Brown, Zora, 60
Bryant, J.S., 75
Buler, B.F., 18
Burch, F.M., 1
Burns, Edith, 57
Burns, G.W., 57

Burns, George W., 87
Burroge, J.C., 12
Burroge, J.E., 21
Burt, John A., 17

C

Caldwell, B.I., 20
Caldwell, T.O., 20
Calvert, James, 47
Calvert, Joseph, 47
Calvert, Mable, 47
Calvert, Parmelia, 47
Cameron, E.D., 46
Campbell, Archibald
  S., 84
Campbell, C.W., 73
Campbell, Elizabeth,
  73
Campbell, H.B., 49
Cannon, Hattie, 58
Cannon, J.S., 58
Capshaw, M.T.J., 22,
  53
Carder, Frederick, 43,
  64, 74, 79, 82
Carder, Nancy E., 64
Carleton, Henry M., 1,
  34
Carlock, Andrew M.,
  30
Carlock, C.M., 36
Carlock, James A., 36
Carlock, Jane, 76

Carlock, Luella, 30
Carnahan, S.P., 75
Carr Salon, 49
Carr, Eva, 37
Carr, Eva A., 42
Carr, W.H., 21, 42, 49
Carrico, M.W., 87
Carrico, Mary E., 87
Carson, J.M., 7
Carter, Frederick, 34,
  40
Carter, Julia A., 19, 21
Cartwright, L.J., 11,
  13
Cartwright, Mary J.,
  11
Caruthers, F., 36, 62,
  69
Caruthers, T., 67
Carver, John F., 51
Cashen, J.C., 90
Cathey, J.W., 64
Cathey, W.W., 67
Cease, Frank P., 3, 49,
  53
Cease, Frank R., 6
Cease, Minnie C., 53
Chapman, L.C., 73
Chapman, W.L., 72
Chastain, J.M., 10, 81
Chastaine, J.M., 43
Chesney, S.O., 1
Chilson, V.B., 2
Chilson, W.D., 2, 3

94

Dye, Thomas, 39

E

Easton, D.B., 62
Easton, Ellen G., 8, 13
Easton, Henry C., 8,
   13
Eaton, Irene P., 88
Eaton, S.A.D., 88
Edwards, L.J., 45
Edwards, R.J., 81
Elder, J.H., 17
Elgin, Charles H., 6,
   14
Elkin, Mattie B., 47
Elkins, Charles, 42, 57
Elkins, George, 15, 42
Elkins, J.A., 14
Elkins, James, 15, 89
Elkins, Mattie B., 42,
   57, 58
Elland, E., 67
Elledge, J.B., 90
Elledge, Nora, 67
Elledge, Tenie, 90
Elledge, W.N., 67
Elledge, William N.,
   87
Ellidge, W.N., 37
Elliott, T.B., 19, 26
Elvington, A.N., 44
Emmons, J.B., 14
Emmons, Mollie C.,

   14
Erwin, Oliver T., 45
Eslich, John I., 4
Eslick, J.W., 50
Eslick, John, 2
Eslick, John I., 61
Eslick, Lizzie, 50
Essex, Frank W., 66
Essex, John, 24
Estate of James
   Calvert, dec'd, 47
Estate of James
   Fitzgerald, 54
Estate of John
   Branhan, 3
Estill, Tuen, 7
Ewart, R.J., 57
Exleton, Amelia, 77
Exleton, E.T., 77

F

Faris, Joseph A., 78
Faris, Sallie T., 78
Fawcett, N.E., 71
Felkner, C.H., 49
Felkner, P.E., 49
Fenelon, John H., 16
Fenelon, Mary, 16
Ferguson, John H., 85,
   89
Ferguson, Nannie E.,
   89
Ferguson, William H.,

Gray, Arena, 83
Gray, J.F., 59
Gray, John F., 83
Green, C.M., 79
Green, Grant, 74
Green, Mrs. May, 85
Green, S.S., 85
Gribble, Mrs. M.F., 74
Grier, William, 33
Griffin, Exa, 12
Griffin, Thomas, 12
Grigsby, Elizabeth J.,
   28
Grigsby, J.D., 2, 28
Grigsby, J.E., 18, 28
Grimmett, H., 55
Grimmett, M., 55
Grimstead, G.C., 70
Grisby, J.E., 43
Grove, Michael B., 11
Groy, Robert F., 75
Gwynne, Llew, 80
Gwynne, Llewelyn, 75
Gysett, John, 46

H

Haas, R.P., 35
Haas, Reuben, 47
Haas, Reuben P., 84
Haddix, Ellen A., 85
Haddix, Martha F., 15
Hales, George H., 7
Hales, Mary F., 7

Hall, Abe, 50, 51, 52
Hall, J.H., 82
Hall, J.M., 68
Hall, John W., 82
Hall, Mrs. S.E., 44
Hall, Survilla E., 78
Hallmark, W.A., 55
Hamilton, J.C., 33, 75
Hamilton, Mary C., 33
Hamilton, May, 75
Hann, J.P.N., 48
Hann, Vastie, 48
Harding, Charles A.,
   56
Harding, Mary M., 56
Hardrick, William, 13
Hardwick, H.M., 89
Hardwick, William, 3
Harrington, C.A., 55
Harris, S.H., 15, 70
Harriss, W.J., 46
Hart, W.H., 67
Harvey, J.R., 54
Hasness, James, 66
Hawk, A.D., 33
Hawk, Alfred D., 34
Hawk, Lucy W., 34
Haws, A.D., 56
Haws, F.W., 13
Hay, Daniel, 2, 9, 16,
   17, 26
Hays, W.W., 51
Helm, Elmer C., 16
Hembree, Charles C.,

32
Hembree, Rosa, 32
Hendricks, T.W., 19,
    24, 26, 27
Hendricks, Victoria,
    24, 26, 27
Hennessy, E.E., 2, 7,
    54, 77
Herronymus. Sallie T.,
    79
Hewett, N.F., 59
Hewitt, Lee D., 62
Hill, John D., 37
Hill, Richard, 6
Hillman, Hugh H., 40,
    63
Hocken, James W., 42
Hocken, Walter E., 42
Hocker, James W., 32,
    48
Hocker, W.E., 58
Hocker, Walter E., 34
Hodam, F.T., 50, 51,
    52
Hodges, John, 56
Hodges, Ollie, 84
Hoffmann, August, 51
Hoover, M.D., 18
Hoovers, M.D., 19
Hoovers, S.C., 19
Hope, R.S., 27
Hope, Sarah B., 27
Horn, William H., 16,
    17

Houghton, T.R., 85
House, George B., 48
Howard, George H., 6
Howarth, M.L., 55
Howry, John H., 84
Hudson, L.P., 11
Hudson, Louis P., 11
Hudson, Sarah J., 11
Hughes, John H., 82
Hughs, William H., 50
Hull, D.H., 4
Hunter, A.T., 15, 16,
    23
Hunter, C.E., 55
Huron, E.E., 14
Hutchin, A., 11, 78

I

Inbody, Ephraim, 31
Inbody, Mindia, 31
Inbody, Samuel, 31
Ingram, Elvira, 78
Ingram, J.H., 78
Innis, Etta M., 89
Innis, Robert E., 6, 89
Isbell, John, 14
Isom, W.M., 59, 71

J

Jackson, J.M., 43, 67
Jackson, J.P., 6, 10,
    43, 81

100

Jackson, John M., 20
Jackson, Minnie, 20,
  43
James, Emily, 46
James, James M., 46
Jameson, B.F., 31
Jasper, James R., 50
Jeffers, Raymond, 78
Jennings, Amanda J.,
  14
Jennings, Lyndal C.,
  37
Jennings, R.H., 6
Jennison Bros. & Co.,
  29
Jennison, A.B., 28
Jennison, Mrs. Anna
  E., 29
Jennison, W.R., 28
Jennisson, Harry, 29
Jennisson, William B.,
  29
Johnson, E.B., 37, 89
Johnson, M.F., 38, 46,
  63, 65, 67, 79
Johnson, M.L., 10
Johnson, T.J., 38, 46,
  63, 65, 67, 79
Johnson, W.H., 37, 89
Johnston, G.P., 30
Jones, Dora, 6
Jones, Ed H., 6
Jones, George F., 2
Jones, Hugh, 25

Jones, Hughbert, 48,
  66, 72
Jones, J.A., 46, 48, 66,
  68, 72, 81, 88
Jones, James A., 7, 72
Jones, Mary E., 72
Jones, Minnie M., 2
Jones, Paul, 29
Jones, Sallie, 66, 68,
  72, 88
Joyce, Robert, 2, 8, 17
Judkins, Frances, 37
Judkins, George, 37,
  41
Judkins, Sarah, 41

K

Kavanaugh, W.B., 21
Keener, James L., 38
Keller, E.J., 12, 30,
  71, 74, 75
Keller, Jessie, 75
Kennedy, James, 28
Kernaghan, John A., 1
King, David, 85
King, M.A., 68
King, W.T., 86
Kingkade, Andrew, 84
Kingkade, Lucy T., 84
Kittredge, Emma, 82
Kittredge, John H., 82
Klinglesmith, J.W., 16
Klinglesmith, Sarah,

16

Rennie, Albert, 11, 87
Rennie, Alexander, 87
Reynolds, George T., 36
Rhymes, P.A., 50
Rhymes, Vicenda, 50
Richardson, D.C., 60
Richardson, J.I., 45
Richardson, Nannie, 45
Richardson, T.M., 9, 36, 60 *{see also T.M. Richardson Lumber Co.}*
Richardson, W.C.W., 9, 63
Riggins, W.S., 46
Ritchesom, T.M., 51
Rixse, Ed C., 14
Robert, M.W., 3
Roberts, E.J., 86
Roberts, J.J., 64
Roberts, Nace G., 40
Robertson, Sam B., 66
Robertson, Samuel, 20
Robinson, Elizabeth, 77, 80
Robinson, Ira, 40
Robinson, Nathaniel, 77
Rogers, William, 49
Rollins, T.J., 10
Rood, C.L., 2
Rood, C.Q., 82

Rood, C.S., 3, 6
Rood, Mrs. C.L., 4
Rory, Vallie E., 75
Rose, Jane, 10
Rose, Robert, 2, 10
Ross, A.T., 8, 9, 21
Runyan, Lelia, 68
Runyan, M.C., 1, 26
Runyan, R.M., 68
Rutherford, J.T., 41

S

Sanders, C.R., 64
Sanders, M.C., 64
Sauls, W.D., 35
Saxon, J.W., 59
Saxon, M.W., 59
Saxon, Mattie J., 59
Schmick, E.O., 7
Schmuck, Elizabeth, 33
Schmuck, V.E., 33
School District #4, 40
Schottenkirk, Jay, 33
Sconce, Cassender, 58
Sconce, J. M., 58
Seawell, Emma, 45
Seawell, W.H., 3, 10, 19, 43, 81
Seawell, W.P., 45
Shannon, J.R., 16, 23
Shannon, Martha T., 13

108

110

Index of Places

112

www.ingramcontent.com/pod-product-compliance
Lightning Source LLC
Chambersburg PA
CBHW032324210326
41519CB00058B/5572